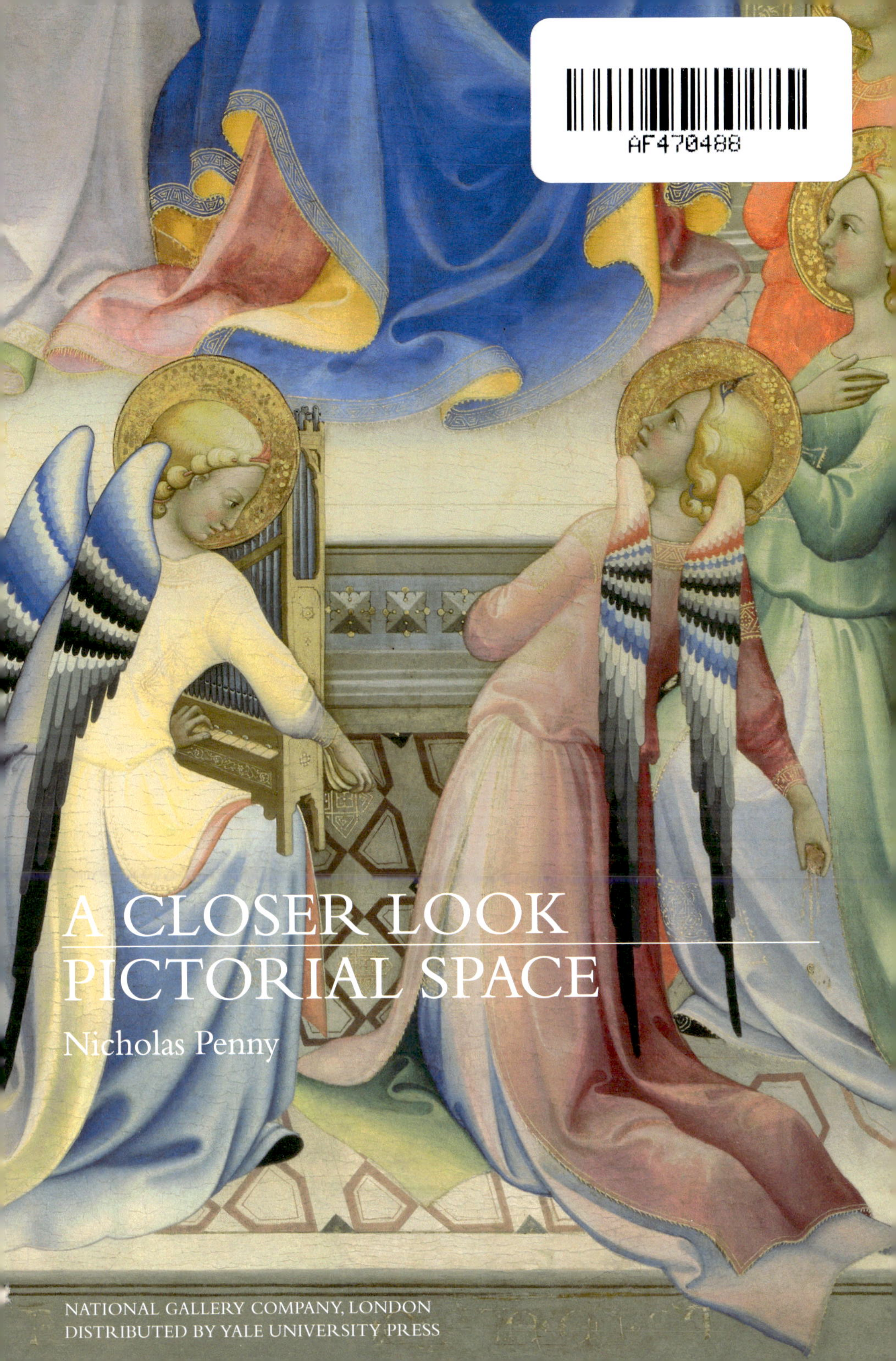

A CLOSER LOOK
PICTORIAL SPACE

Nicholas Penny

NATIONAL GALLERY COMPANY, LONDON
DISTRIBUTED BY YALE UNIVERSITY PRESS

Nicholas Penny was Director of the National Gallery from 2008 to 2015. His publications include three catalogues of the National Gallery's sixteenth-century Italian paintings (the third volume with Giorgia Mancini) and *Frames* in the Closer Look series. He is a regular contributor to the *London Review of Books* and the *Burlington Magazine*. He has published as much on sculpture as on painting, including *The Materials of Sculpture*.

Front cover: Akseli Gallen-Kallela, *Lake Keitele*, 1905, detail.
Title page: Lorenzo Monaco, *Coronation of the Virgin with Saints (The San Benedetto Altarpiece)*, 1407–9, detail.
Contents page: Antonello da Messina, *Saint Jerome in his Study*, about 1475, detail.

Published by National Gallery Company Limited
St Vincent House, 30 Orange Street, London WC2H 7HH
ISBN 978 1 85709 616 3
1043606

10 9 8 7 6 5 4 3 2 1

British Library Cataloguing-in-Publication Data
A catalogue record is available from the British Library
Library of Congress Catalog Card Number: 2016960992

PUBLISHER Jan Green
PROJECT EDITOR Sarah Derry
DESIGNER Raymonde Watkins
PRODUCTION Jane Hyne and Amanda Mackie
Printed and bound in Hong Kong by Printing Express Ltd

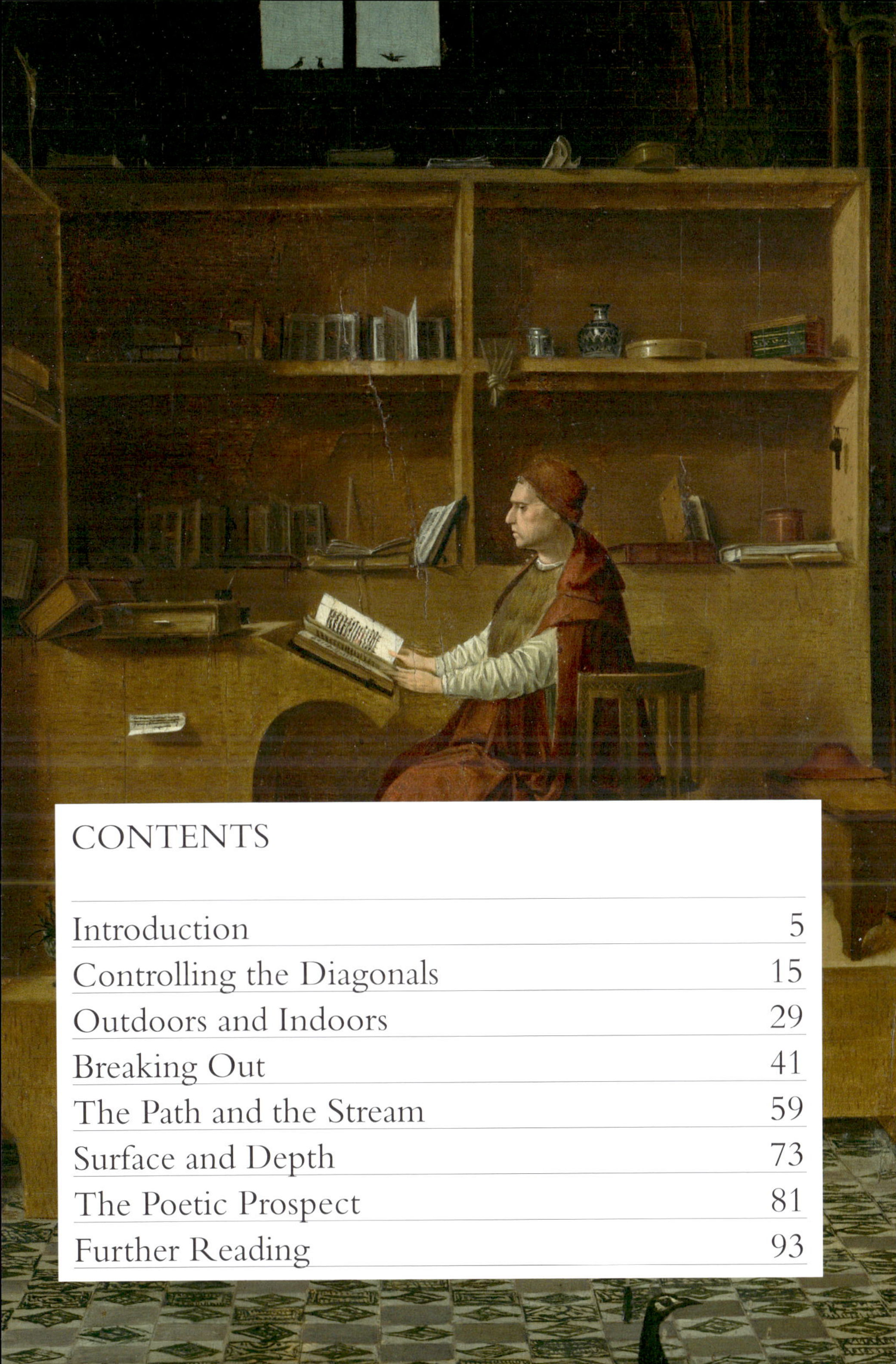

CONTENTS

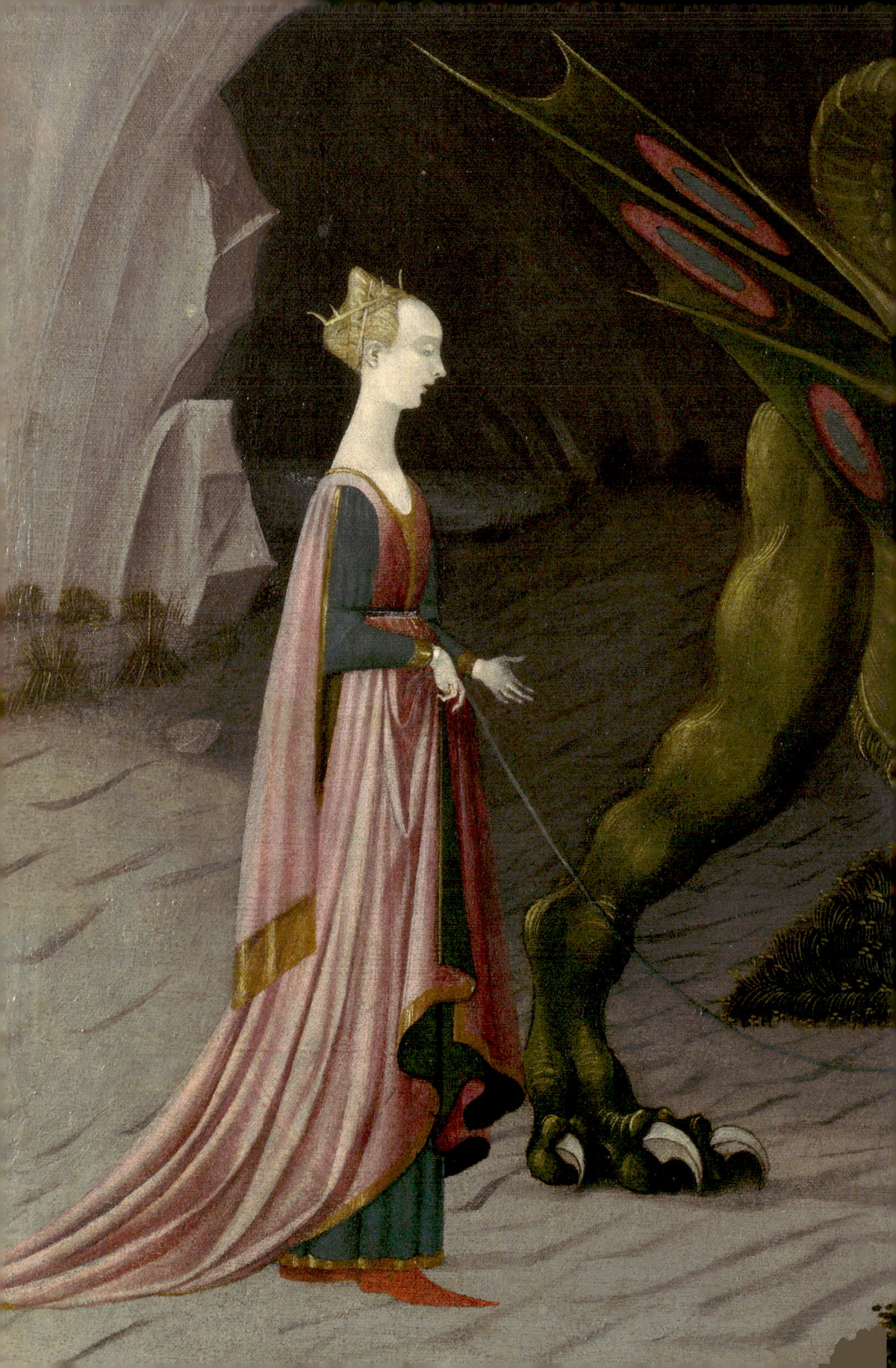

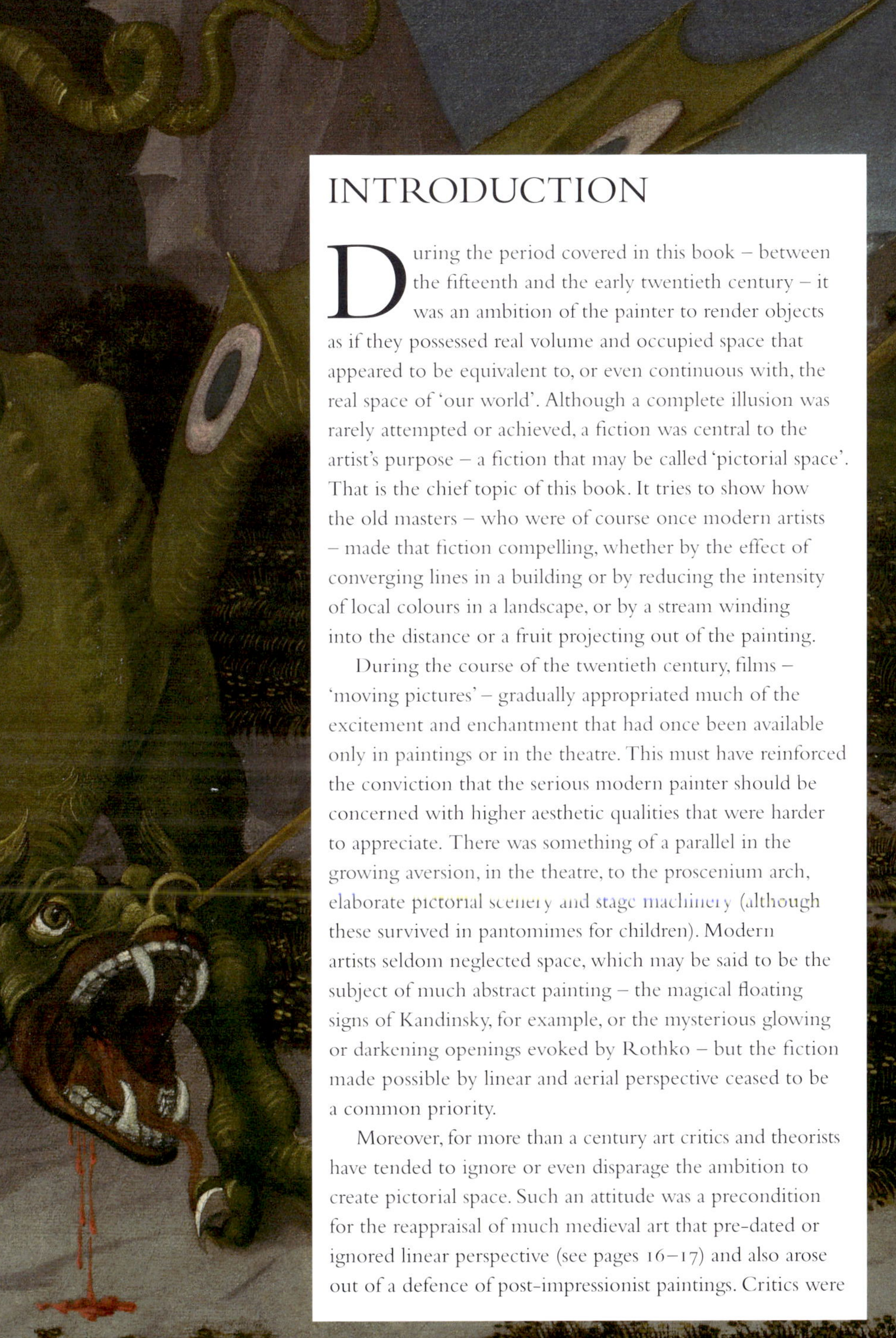

INTRODUCTION

During the period covered in this book – between the fifteenth and the early twentieth century – it was an ambition of the painter to render objects as if they possessed real volume and occupied space that appeared to be equivalent to, or even continuous with, the real space of 'our world'. Although a complete illusion was rarely attempted or achieved, a fiction was central to the artist's purpose – a fiction that may be called 'pictorial space'. That is the chief topic of this book. It tries to show how the old masters – who were of course once modern artists – made that fiction compelling, whether by the effect of converging lines in a building or by reducing the intensity of local colours in a landscape, or by a stream winding into the distance or a fruit projecting out of the painting.

During the course of the twentieth century, films – 'moving pictures' – gradually appropriated much of the excitement and enchantment that had once been available only in paintings or in the theatre. This must have reinforced the conviction that the serious modern painter should be concerned with higher aesthetic qualities that were harder to appreciate. There was something of a parallel in the growing aversion, in the theatre, to the proscenium arch, elaborate pictorial scenery and stage machinery (although these survived in pantomimes for children). Modern artists seldom neglected space, which may be said to be the subject of much abstract painting – the magical floating signs of Kandinsky, for example, or the mysterious glowing or darkening openings evoked by Rothko – but the fiction made possible by linear and aerial perspective ceased to be a common priority.

Moreover, for more than a century art critics and theorists have tended to ignore or even disparage the ambition to create pictorial space. Such an attitude was a precondition for the reappraisal of much medieval art that pre-dated or ignored linear perspective (see pages 16–17) and also arose out of a defence of post-impressionist paintings. Critics were

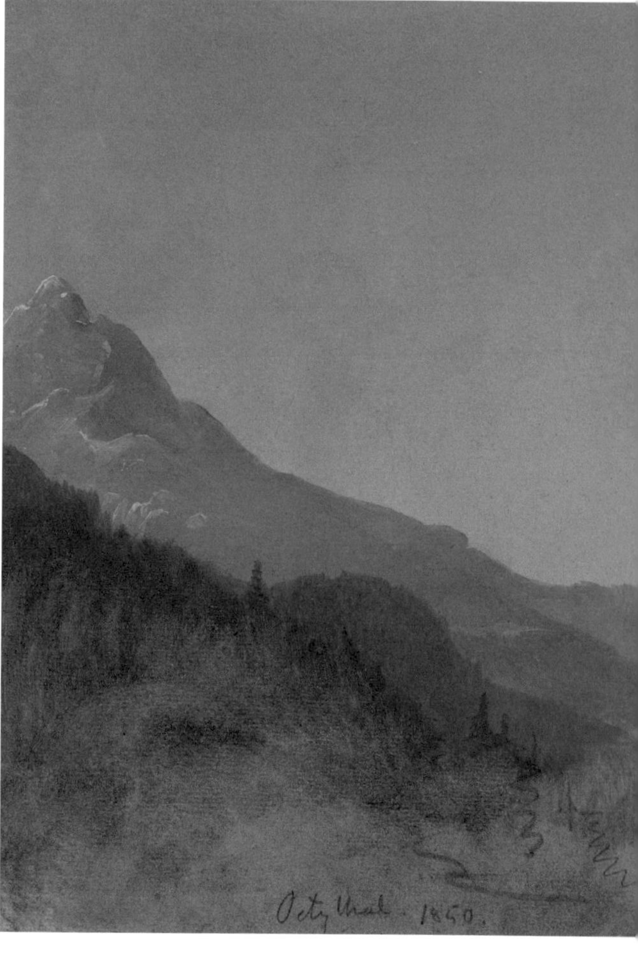

1. Vilhelm Petersen, *Oetzhal*, 1850. This oil sketch was made in the open air. Such studies, typically on paper, often had unfinished foregrounds and were annotated in pencil.

Previous pages: Paolo Uccello, *Saint George and the Dragon*, about 1470, detail.

also influenced by the competing attractions of photography and, surely, as mentioned already, by movies. It has become rare for educated art lovers to exclaim that a painting seems marvellously real, that a portrait might almost speak, or that fur was so well rendered that it might be stroked. Such reactions now seem naive. And yet in the past the most sophisticated connoisseurs made claims of this kind, which indeed artists hoped to elicit.

Aerial perspective can be explained in scientific terms, but an understanding of 'molecular scattering' and 'veiling luminescence' would not necessarily enhance our ability to respond to, or record, the progressive fading of colours and the growing indistinctness of form as objects recede into the distance, or

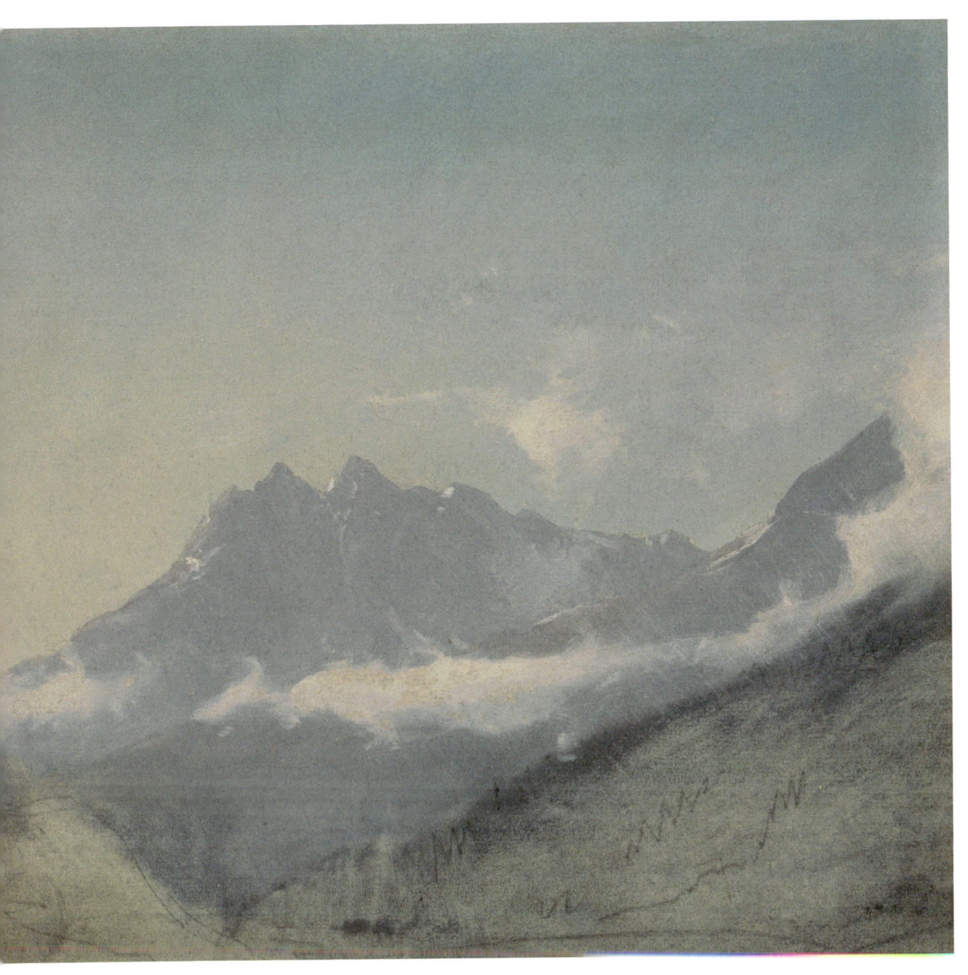

the way that the colour of hills, which we know to be green, appears to be blue or violet grey from a distance. Quick sketches made out of doors were an obvious way to study these rapidly changing effects. Most such sketches that survive – and probably most that were ever made – date from the late eighteenth or nineteenth centuries. A fine example is a view in the Austrian Alps that was painted on paper by the young Danish artist Vilhelm Petersen on his way to Italy in September 1850 [1]. The artist has omitted the foreground. The middle distance is roughly indicated in pencil. Beyond the peaks of the pines on the left the mountains are recorded in shades of lilac grey with vertical brushstrokes for the nearer slopes where forest can just be discerned. The light clouds on the right in front of the

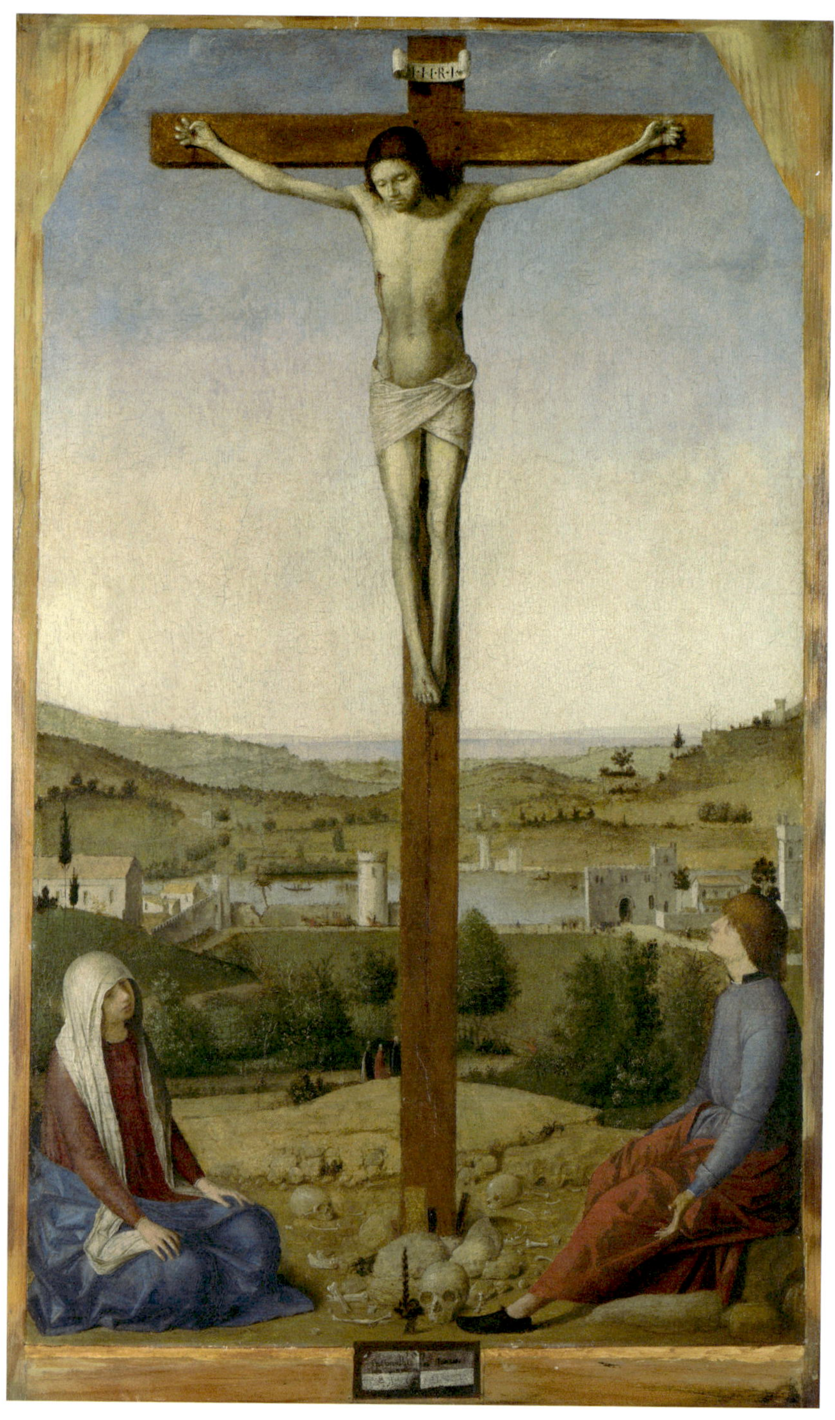

mountain must have moved and perhaps dispersed before the sketch was finished, or abandoned.

Petersen would be surprised to discover that his sketch was ever framed, let alone displayed in the National Gallery, since he made it as a study that might be referred to later when he needed to paint a more finished landscape. Alpine scenery was of special interest in the mid-nineteenth century, when mountain walking and climbing had become popular, but extensive panoramas, often including distant mountains, first appeared in European paintings during the fifteenth century. Antonello da Messina, at work in the 1470s, is unlikely to have made sketches on paper but he must certainly have made mental notes of an equivalent kind in order to paint the landscape in his Crucifixion [2], which extends from the foot of Golgotha, the hill on which the cross has been erected. The figures below the hill are already very small. Beyond them there is a meadow, then the white walls and tidy buildings of a port overlooking a strip of calm water, followed by a succession of gentle hills extending to the distant sea [3]. The tranquil beauty of this scene and the soft transitions of colour and light, especially in the sky as it fades from blue to white before meeting the blue of the sea, contrasts with the sorrowful attitudes of the Virgin Mary and Saint John in the foreground. They seem almost pressed against the frame to make room for the artist's native Sicily which extends beneath Christ's feet and may be understood as a beneficiary of his sacrifice.

The rendering of the landscape, with its many miniature features and its vibrant light, is indebted to Antonello's study of Netherlandish painting from the point of view of both subject and technique. It thrills us with its realism yet it also provides a pleasure that belongs entirely to art. Whereas in life we may look far into the distance, straining to see someone

> *… till the diminution*
> *Of space had pointed him sharp as my needle;*
> *Nay, follow'd him, till he had melted from*
> *The smallness of a gnat to air …*

we would not be aware of much else, even if we are looking at the setting sun, rather than someone we love (as in these lines from Shakespeare's *Cymbeline*). But in a painting our focus can encompass both near and far, and consider relationships between – for example – the jawbone in the foreground and the crenellations of the city wall in the distance.

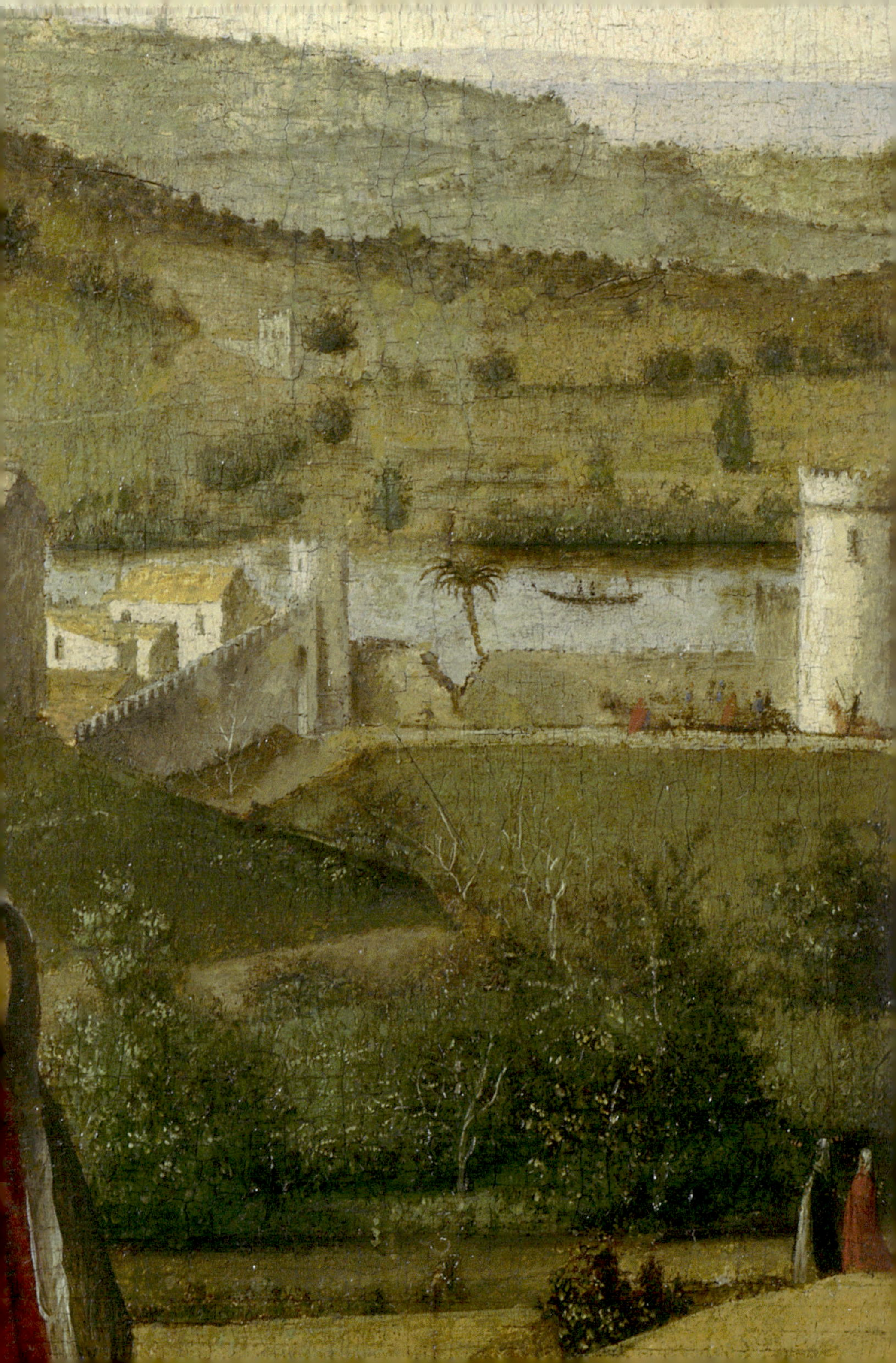

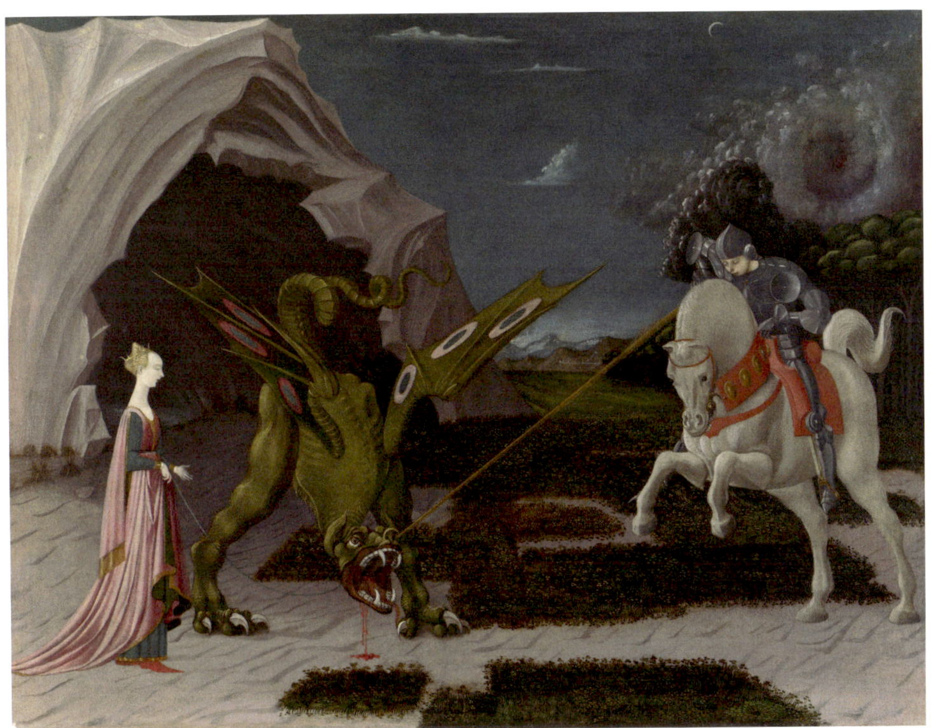

3. Enlarged detail from *Christ Crucified*. The tremulous quality of the sunlight is enhanced by the ragged edges of the distant hillside. The identity of the three processing figures, lower right, is uncertain, as is the identity of the figures riding by the city wall.

4. Paolo Uccello, *Saint George and the Dragon*, about 1470.

Linear perspective is a device for representing in two dimensions some basic aspects of our visual experience, notably the apparent diminution of objects which are identical in size, and the apparent convergence of lines we know to be parallel. It is of great practical use, for example in explaining how to assemble machinery or helping us envisage an architect's design, and it is of central importance for anyone exploring how our eyes work, as well as a means whereby artists create pictorial space. Artists working in the European tradition have usually adopted a system in which there is one point, known as the vanishing point, towards which all the parallel lines in the picture converge, but there are other systems in which there is more than one vanishing point, and many artists have chosen to improvise in an unsystematic way.

Paolo Uccello's small painting of Saint George and the Dragon [4] is disturbing and very unusual in its treatment of the subject, since the monster that George lances in the eye has already been tamed by the princess, a delicate creature, shown in profile, with her pale face and hands contrasted with the dark vaulted aperture of the cave from which her horrid pet has emerged. But the figure of the saint on his rearing steed reflects the artist's fascination with foreshortening – the technical term for delineating solids so that they appear to recede. An example of this would be the arm of a man pointing at the beholder so that the hand seems unusually large and the arm has mostly disappeared; or a horse seen from behind, or from in front, or – as here – at an angle [5]. The curvature of the neck and tail of Uccello's horse reveals how the artist strove to separate anatomical parts and treat each as a geometric unit (the saint's plate armour already has such a geometrical character). Saint George resembles a placid schoolboy but his horse is fierce and Uccello has taken great trouble to depict both its upper and lower teeth. Behind the saint there is a sort of tornado or spiralling wind tunnel resting on darker clouds, and also a dense forest of schematic trees. The tunnel curving back into space echoes the ribbed interior of the dragon's cave. It is also a dynamic geometric puzzle. It was said that when Uccello showed his good friend the great Florentine sculptor Donatello some of the designs he had been working on – spheres cut into seventy-two equal facets and shavings coiling around sticks – the sculptor lamented that they were only fit to be ornaments for inlaid decoration (where they are indeed found). But such exercises, which were said to have so fascinated the artist that he was reluctant to go to bed, surely had some influence on his painting.

When we step back from this picture, the most compelling spatial indicator within it is the long diagonal of Saint George's lance. Linear perspective succeeds as a way of organising a composition, and of defining pictorial space, in paintings that include more of such diagonals – especially when these are the parallel lines of a building that appear to converge. The great impression made in Florence by Uccello's lost mural painting of the Annunciation was still remembered over a century later. It included the depiction of a building, the extent of which really deceived the eye to a degree that no one had previously experienced. The painting does not survive but it established a convention whereby the subject of the Annunciation provided a pretext for virtuoso perspectival performances.

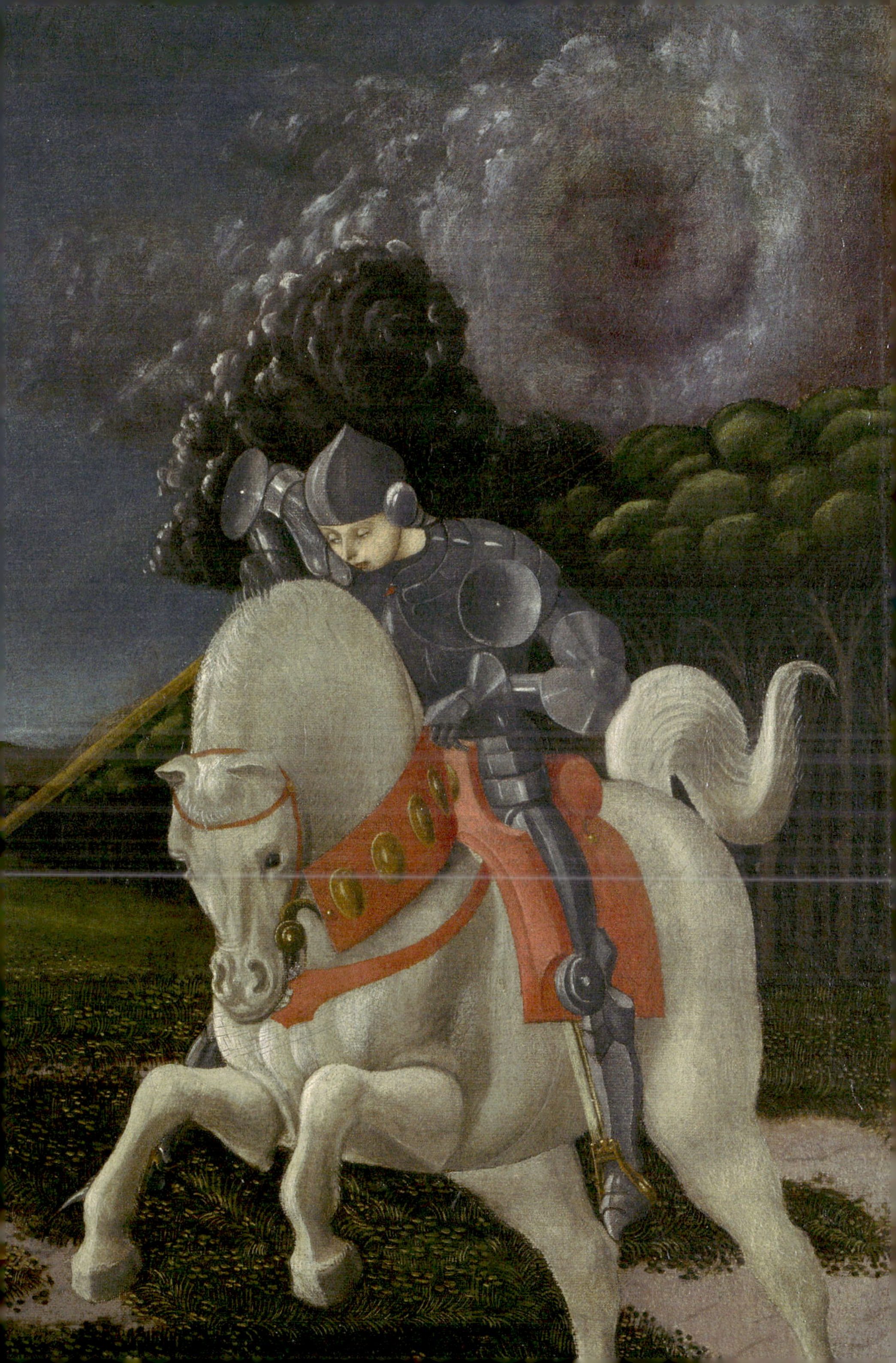

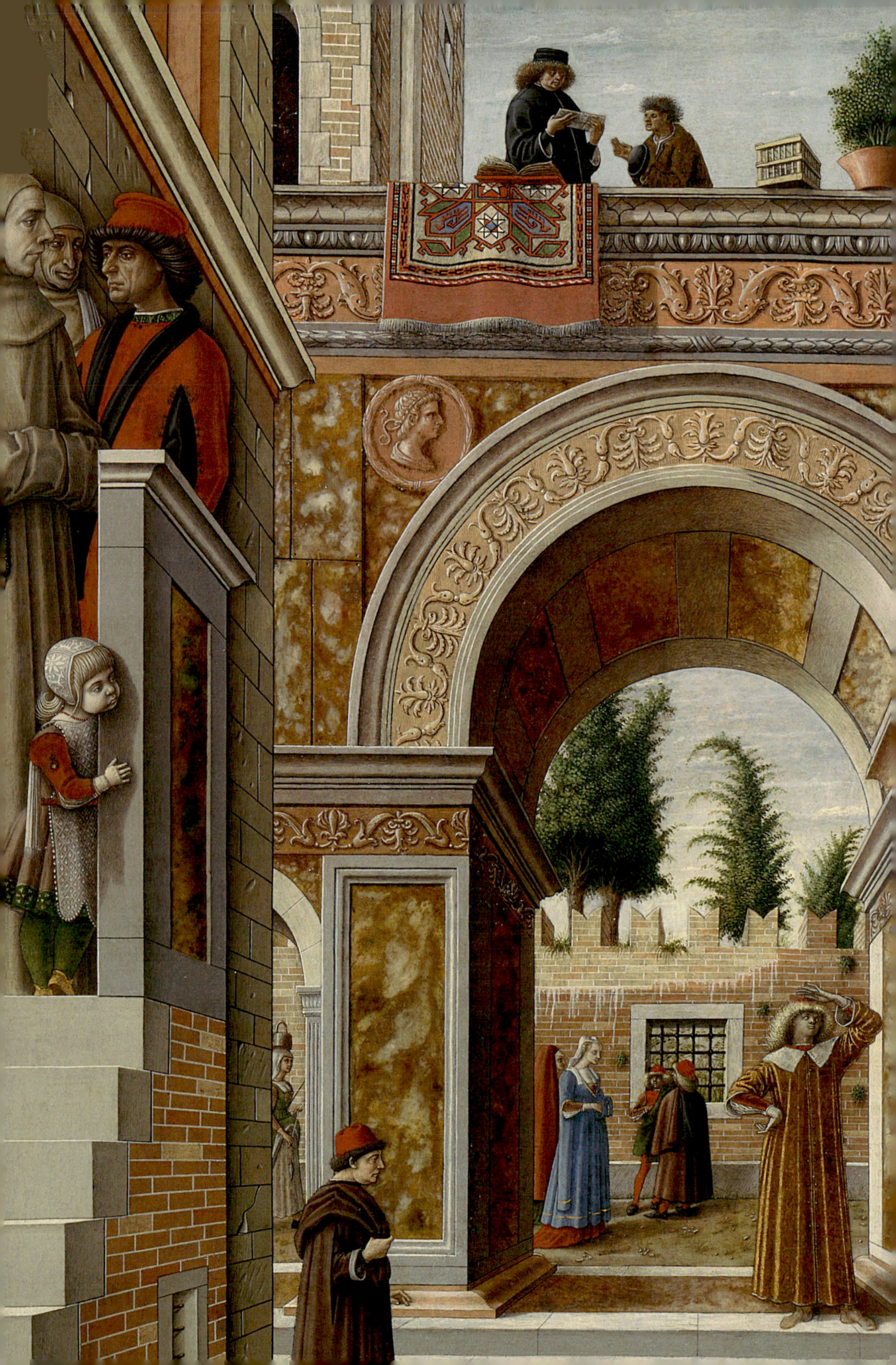

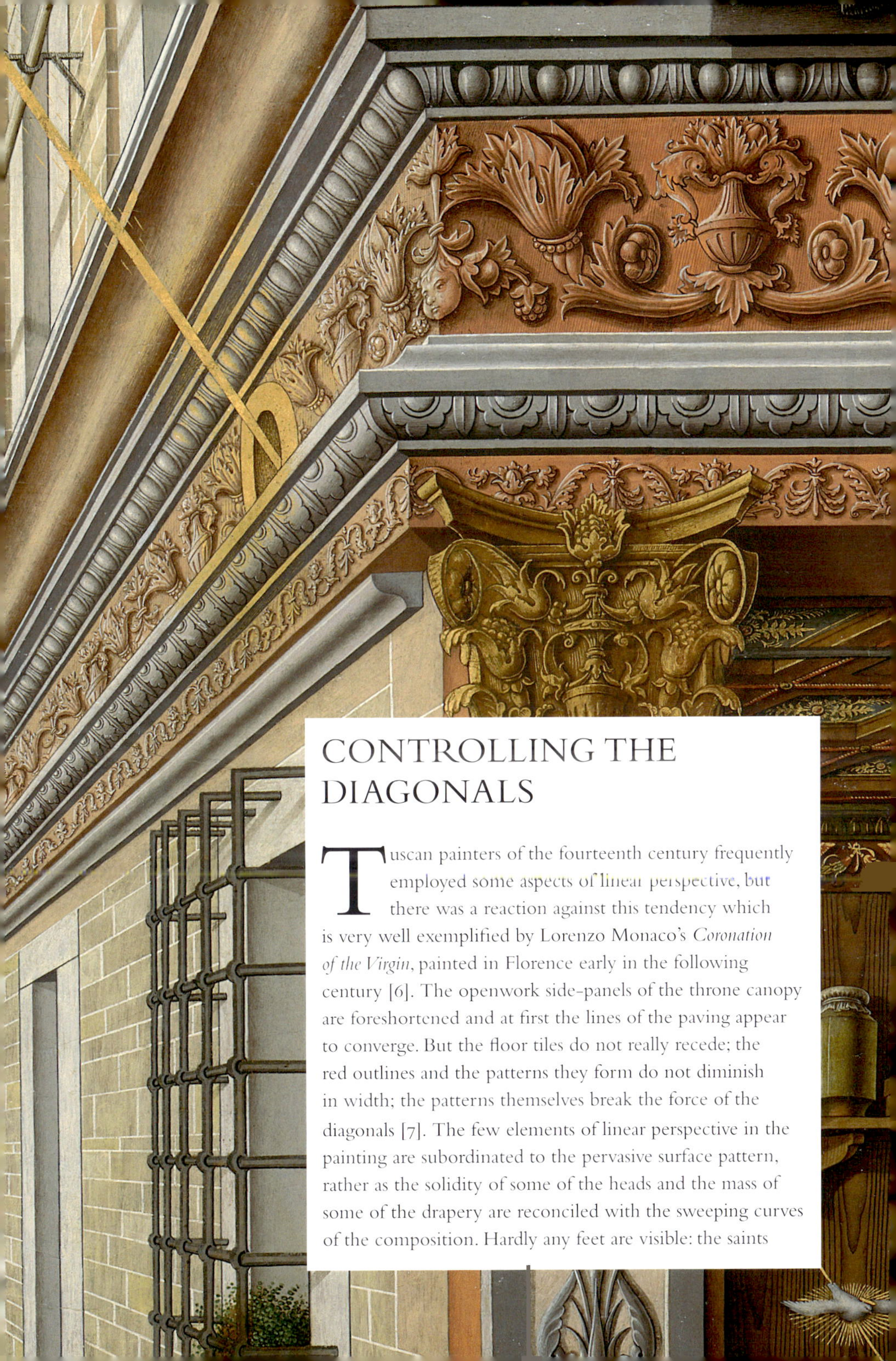

CONTROLLING THE DIAGONALS

Tuscan painters of the fourteenth century frequently employed some aspects of linear perspective, but there was a reaction against this tendency which is very well exemplified by Lorenzo Monaco's *Coronation of the Virgin*, painted in Florence early in the following century [6]. The openwork side-panels of the throne canopy are foreshortened and at first the lines of the paving appear to converge. But the floor tiles do not really recede; the red outlines and the patterns they form do not diminish in width; the patterns themselves break the force of the diagonals [7]. The few elements of linear perspective in the painting are subordinated to the pervasive surface pattern, rather as the solidity of some of the heads and the mass of some of the drapery are reconciled with the sweeping curves of the composition. Hardly any feet are visible: the saints

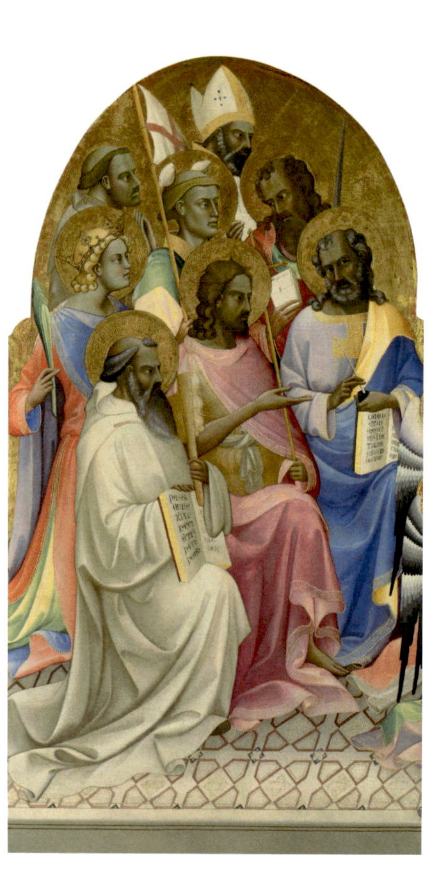
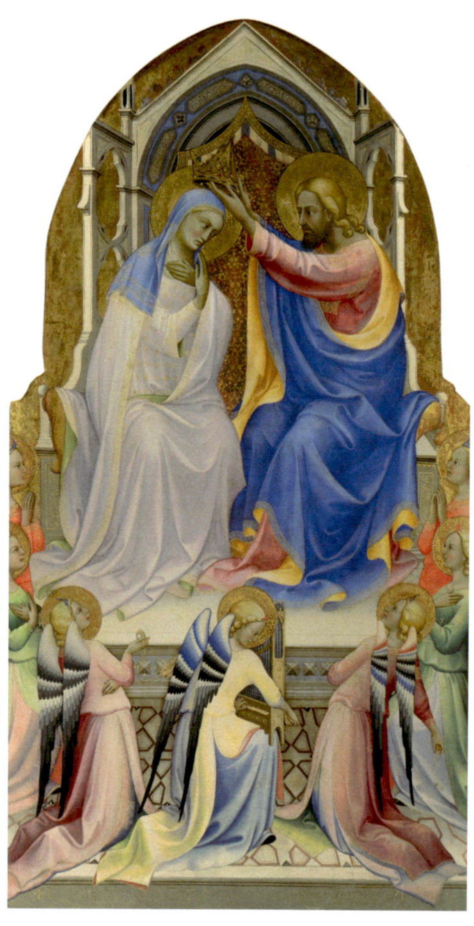

6. Lorenzo Monaco, *Coronation of the Virgin with Saints (The San Benedetto Altarpiece)*, 1407–9.

Previous pages: Carlo Crivelli, *The Annunciation, with Saint Emidius*, 1486, detail.

flanking the throne, although seated, seem to float, as do the kneeling angels. Two rows of saints are standing (although that is not at first obvious) behind the six seated ones. Their heads diminish slightly in size, but also form diagonal patterns on the surface of the painting, rising from the outside corners and then back to the centres of the arches, which are touched by the mitre on the left and the tiara on the right.

Several decades later in Siena, not far from Florence, we find linear perspective being enthusiastically deployed but in a completely unfamiliar way. In Giovanni di Paolo's *Birth of Saint John the Baptist* [8], one of a series of paintings illustrating the life of the saint, arches can be seen beyond arches in the room beyond the one represented. The paving diminishes in size, as do the walls and the headboard of the bed; but the footboard is larger at its further end. The artist has also ensured that the

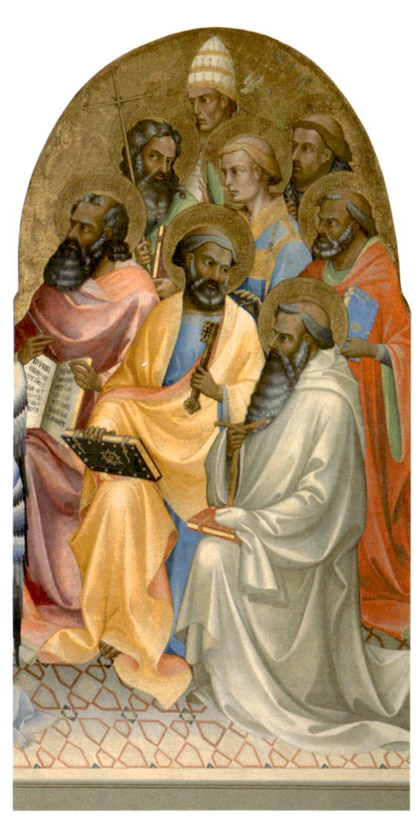

7. Detail from *Coronation of the Virgin with Saints*. The tiles are angled to suggest recession but do not diminish in size. Saint Peter's toes are visible beneath the yellow cloak.

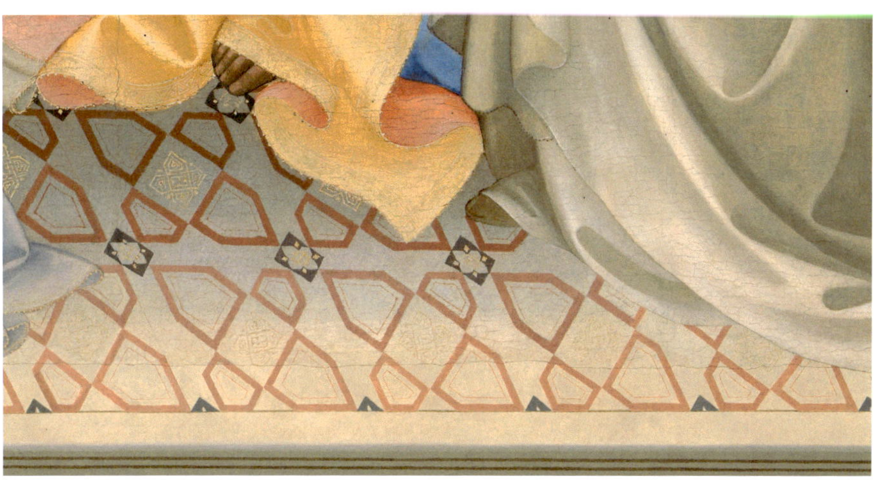

8. Giovanni di Paolo, *The Birth of Saint John the Baptist*, 1454.
The body of the maid warming the cloth by the fire is almost aligned with the receding diagonal of the hearth, and the left leg of the nurse is aligned with the receding lines of the paving. Saint Anne, in the bed, is the same scale as the foreground figures.

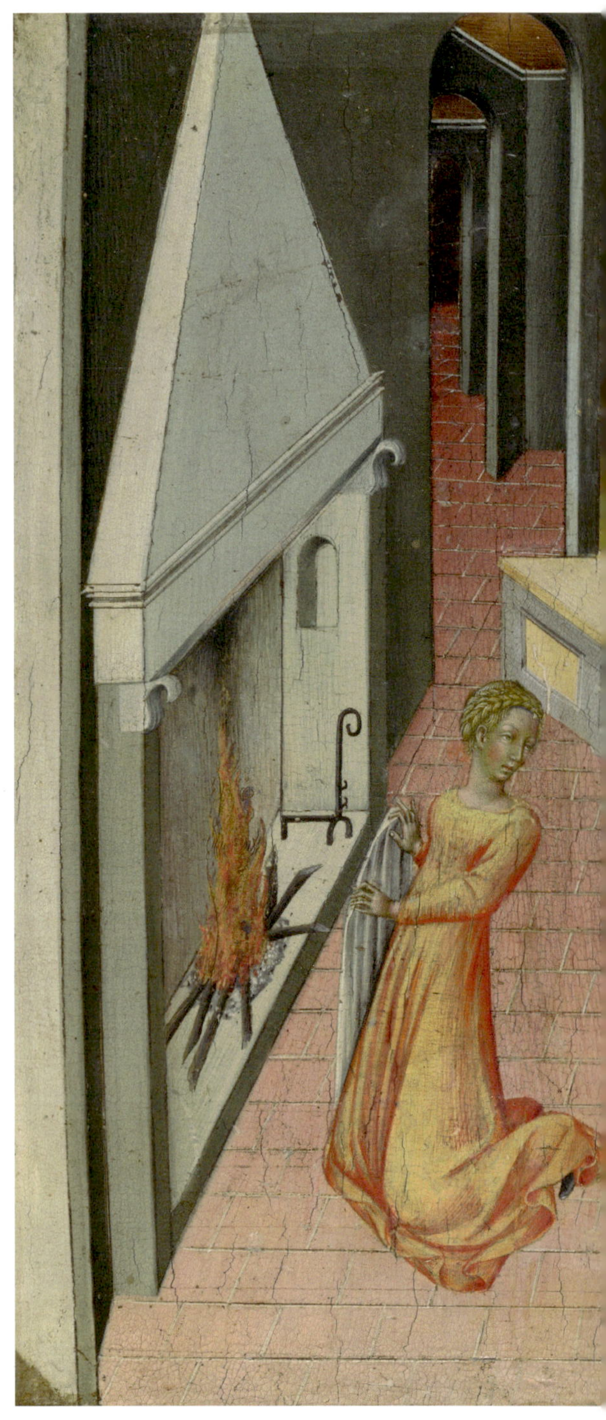

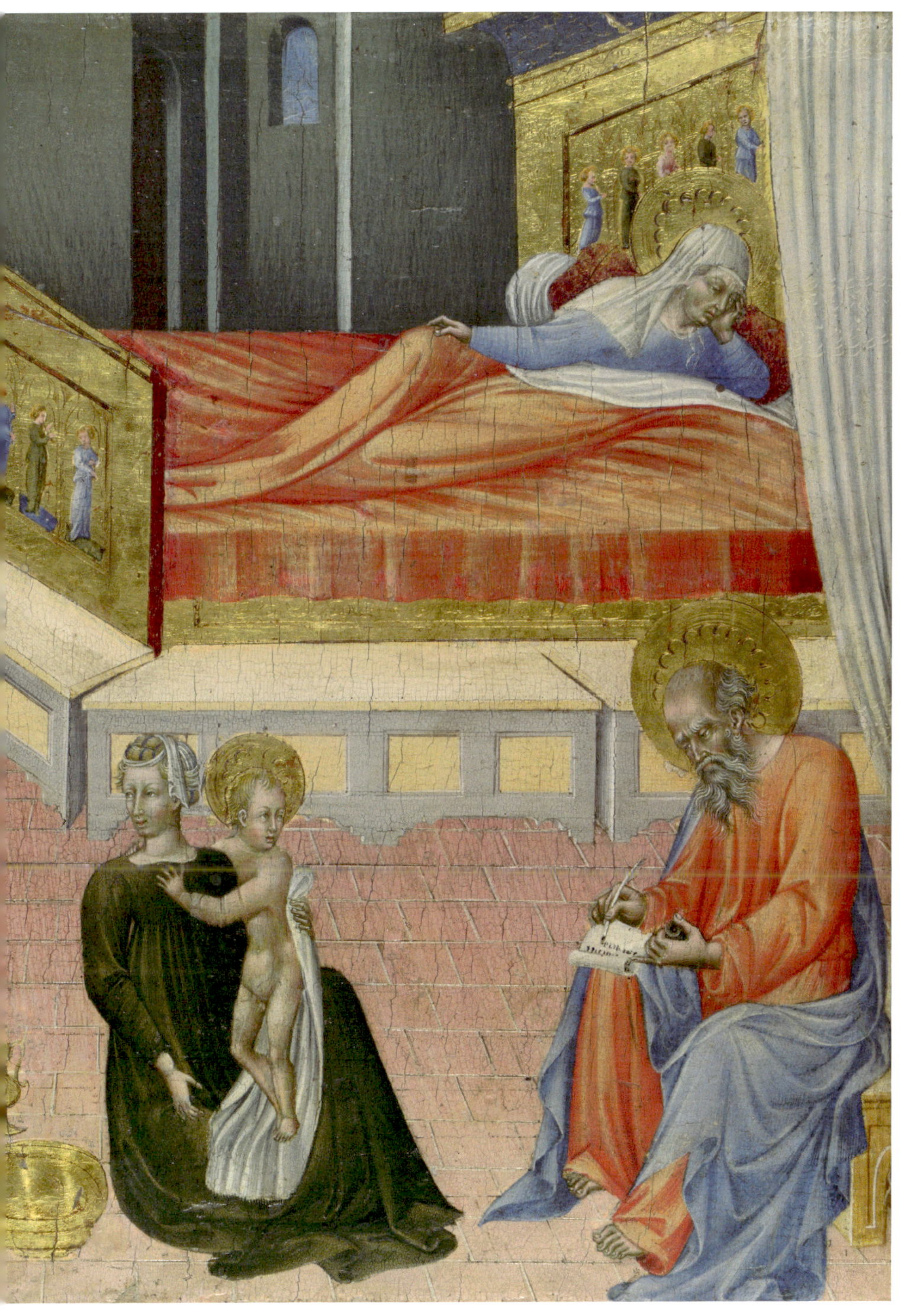

receding parallels do not converge on a single point. Perhaps he felt that it would draw the eye away from the action in the foreground, where Zacharias writes out the name of his newborn son. No one has explained this very unorthodox treatment of space but it certainly cannot be dismissed as mere incompetence.

By contrast, more than twenty years earlier, an artist in Robert Campin's workshop in The Netherlands painted a domestic interior [9], also with a blazing fire and floor tiles (of porphyry, in this case). Here the parallels more or less converge, but the point of convergence is on the extreme left (the composition may originally have been devised as the right-hand wing of a diptych). The Virgin and Child occupy so much of the composition that the receding lines do not distract us for long, and the entire domestic space is unified by light: firelight reflecting on the lintel of the chimney, daylight illuminating the multiple mouldings of each corbel, the hanging cloth casting a double shadow. This painting was made without the benefit of the geometric exercises favoured by Florentine artists such as Uccello.

Half a century later, Crivelli painted the *Annunciation* for the high altar of the Franciscan convent of the Annunziata in Ascoli Piceno [11], and here we experience just how compelling the device of a single vanishing point can be. It is hard enough to discern many of the painting's fine details when seen in a gallery, and impossible to believe that they would have been visible in its original position as an altarpiece in a church. Indeed, the artist has taken special trouble with the parts that would be impossible to appreciate in such a setting: notably, the foreshortening of the brick courses and the openings of the dovecote in the top left corner, and the way the doves are depicted from several angles and performing a variety of actions [10]. What we cannot miss is the very unusual prominence given by Crivelli here and in other paintings to fruit and vegetables – in this case an apple and cucumber – but these will be discussed in a later chapter (pages 50–2).

The Virgin Mary's palatial home is decorated with intricate gilt-bronze capitals, crisply carved stone pilaster-panels, veneers of figured marble and alabaster, and oriental rugs – as well as, rather surprisingly, a lectern and a wall of conifer planking with a bold grain. But the artist's descriptive powers are manifested not only in his attention to materials but also by his foreshortening of complex motifs such as ceiling rosettes and birdcages. The paving and the entablatures and cornices, especially those of Mary's palace, rush us back to the barred window in the distant

9. Workshop of Robert Campin (Jacques Daret?), *The Virgin and Child in an Interior*, before 1432. The double shadow of the hanging cloth is the sort of detail recorded more than two centuries later by Vermeer (see page 38).

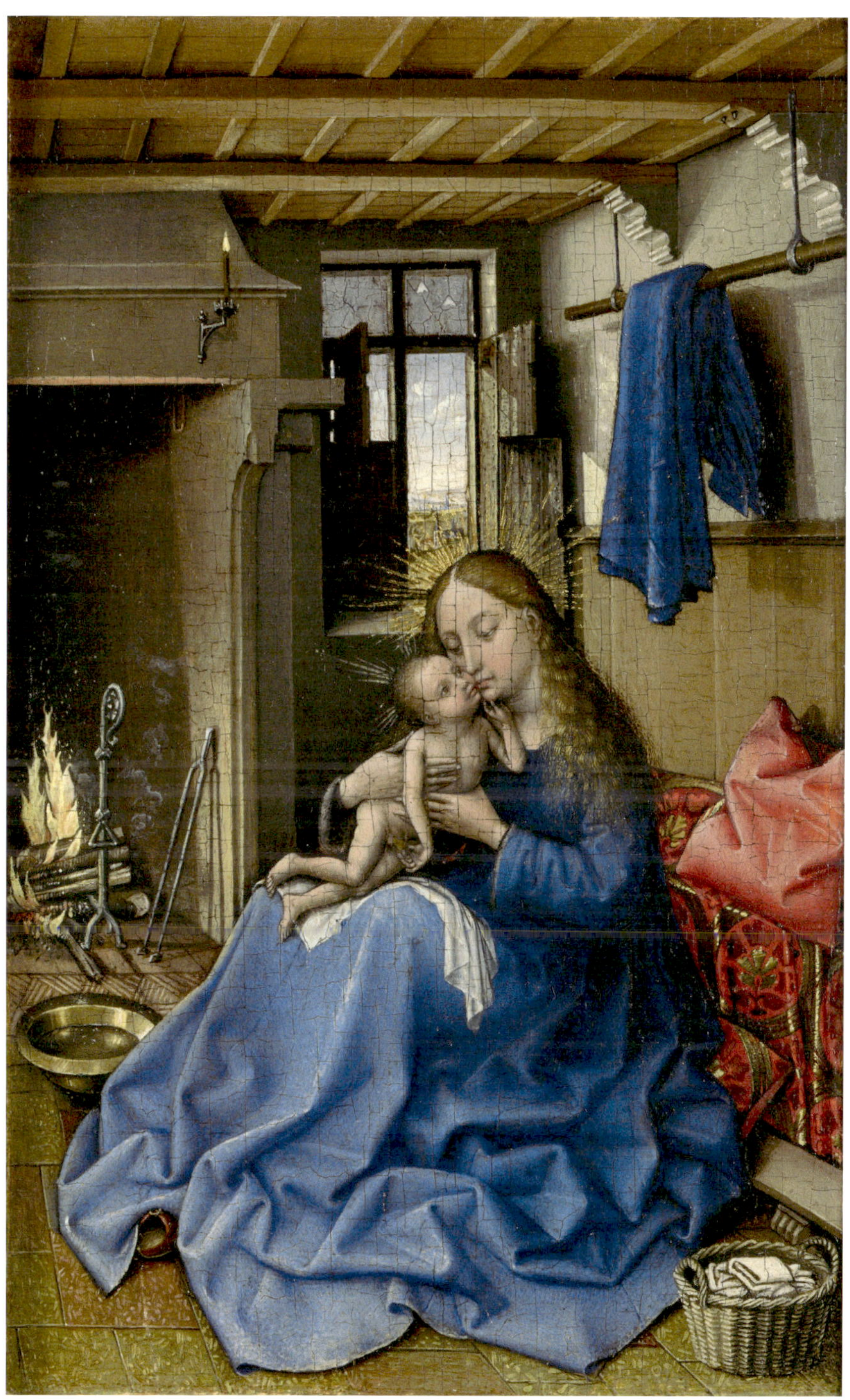

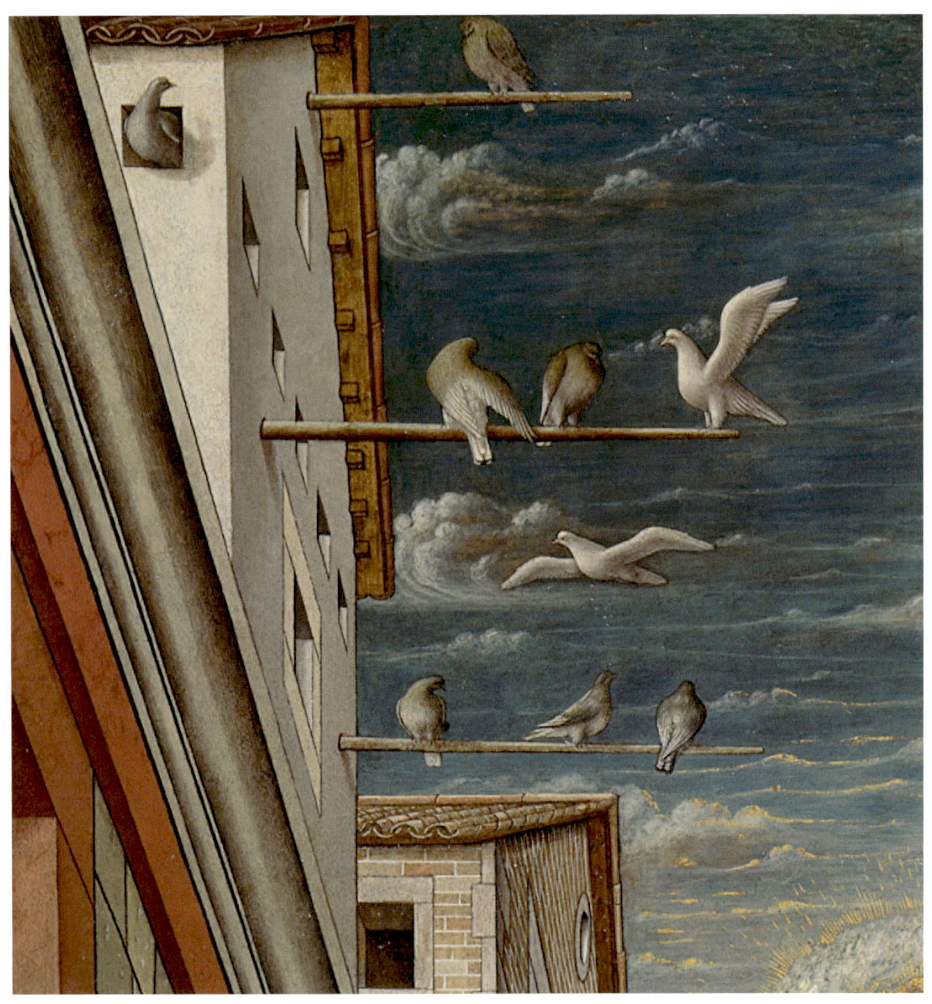

city wall. Crivelli cunningly enables us also to think of this back to front, for the receding lines correspond to the sightline of the dignitary with hand raised to shade his eyes. Moreover, as we follow the street leading into the distance we cross the flight path of the Holy Spirit on its way from the heavens to the Virgin's bedchamber (through a convenient opening in the entablature).

Crivelli would have had a ready reply to any suggestion that his use of perspective distracts attention from his primary subject, that of the Annunciation, for the painting also commemorates the granting by the papacy of a measure of self-government to Ascoli Piceno, which had been declared on the feast day of the Annunciation (and apparently delivered by pigeon post, an event

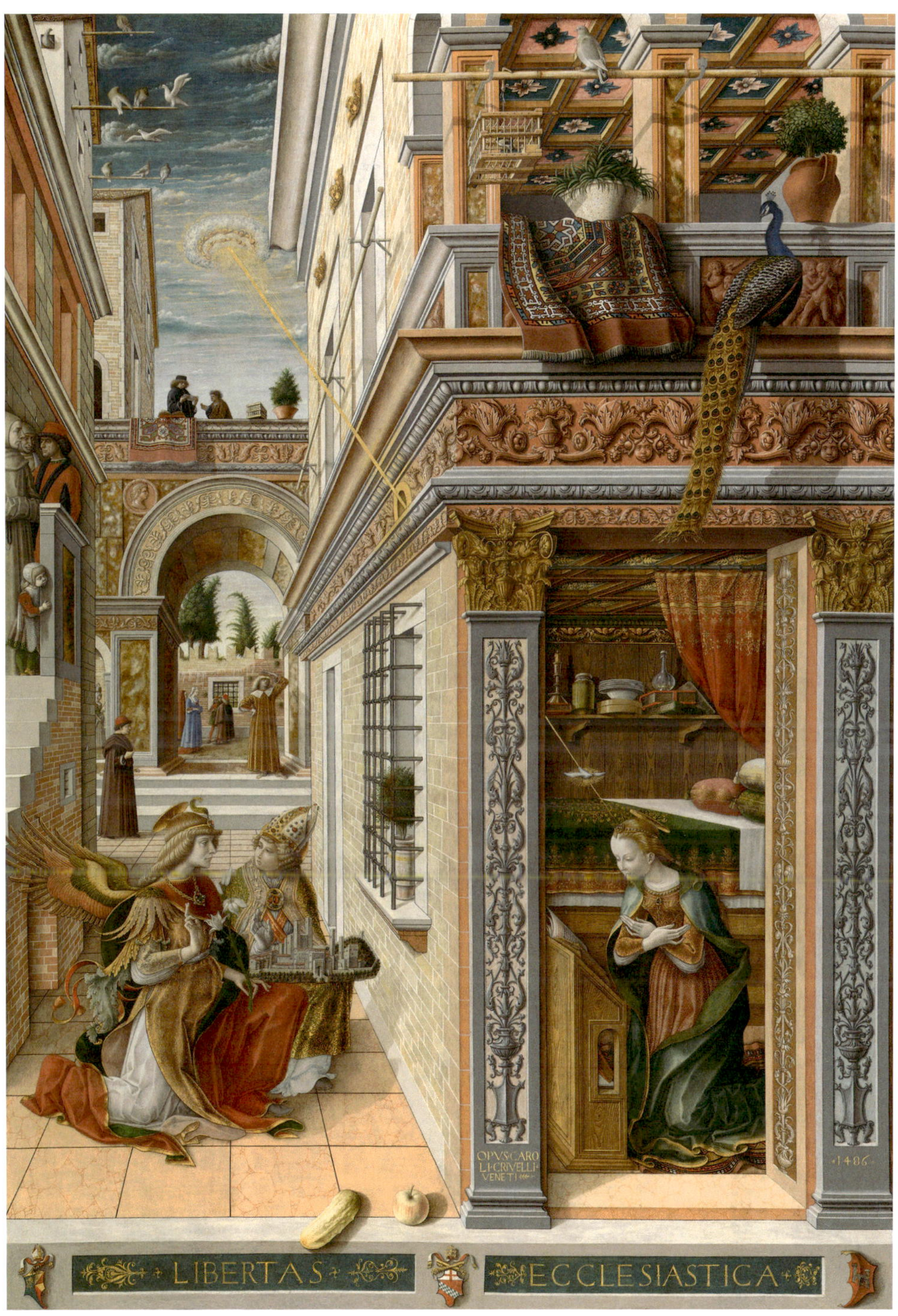

OPVS CARO
LI CRIVELLI
VENETI
1486
LIBERTAS
ECCLESIASTICA

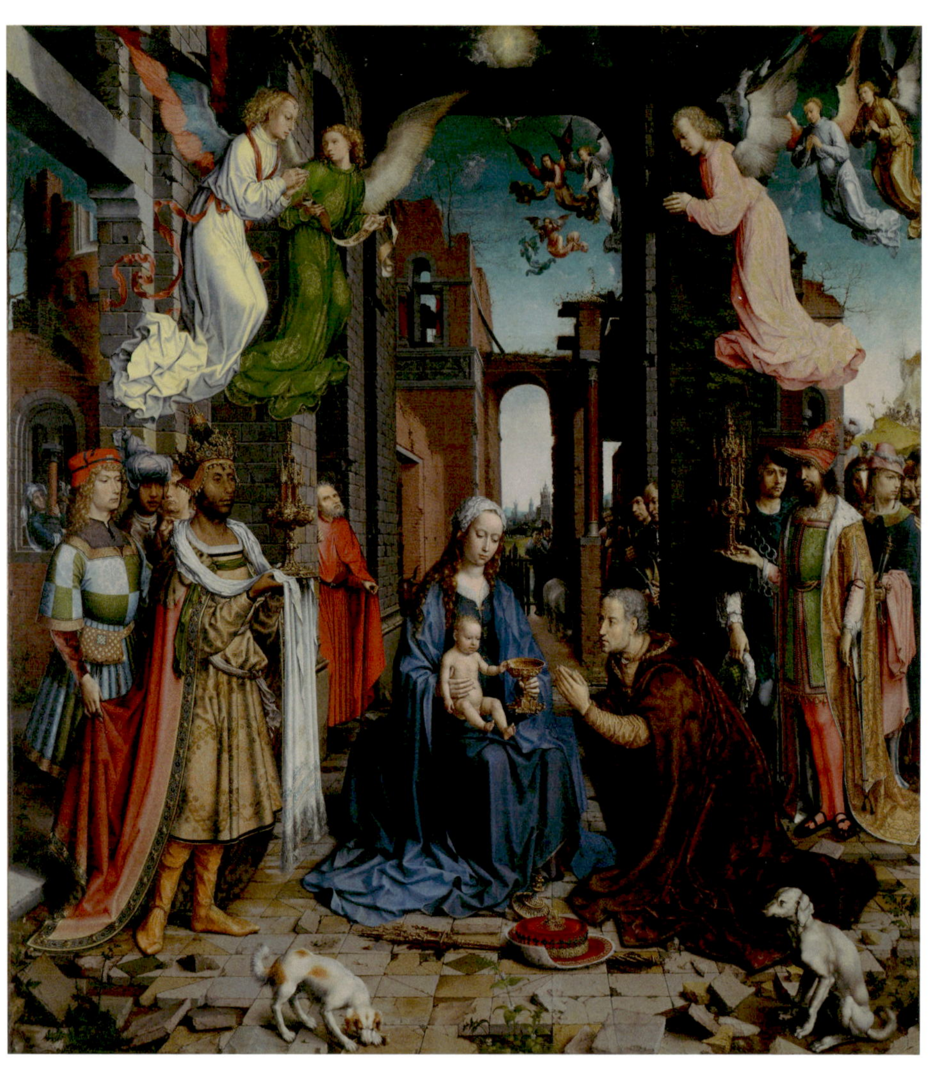

that can be seen on the bridge in the middle distance). The angel Gabriel is accompanied by the city's patron saint, Emidius. They both kneel in the street outside the Virgin's house. Combining two subjects perhaps made a completely unified composition impossible, but the artist's ambition to exhibit his virtuosity was a higher priority than the creation of such unity.

Jan Gossaert's *Adoration of the Kings* [12], painted about twenty-five years later, has a similar richness and diversity of setting and incident. The Virgin Mary and the newborn infant Christ are seated within a ruined palace complex of stone and brick that incorporates exquisite friezes and column shafts of polished semi-precious stone. The sky is divided into eight parts. In one we find the star that has guided the kings and, in another, the Holy Spirit. The eye is detained by minute details: from the weeds among the broken paving-tiles to the spires of the distant city, from the elaborate goldsmith's work of the containers of frankincense and myrrh to the bare extremities of distant trees. The architectural openings are occupied: by Joseph (dressed in red, centre left), by the ox (behind the Virgin Mary's right shoulder), by the innkeeper (on the extreme left) and by numerous curious shepherds. Nevertheless, the receding lines, of ashlar, brick courses, stone lintels and paving, retain their strength [13]. They not only lead into the distance beside and beyond the Virgin's head, where the sky is lightest and dawn begins to break, and where more shepherds peer in from behind a fence [14], but they also serve as diagonal pointers, directing us towards the Virgin herself. It is this calculated combination of spatial recession and surface diagonals that, together with the light, gives Gossaert's painting an extraordinary coherence that was beyond the power of Crivelli.

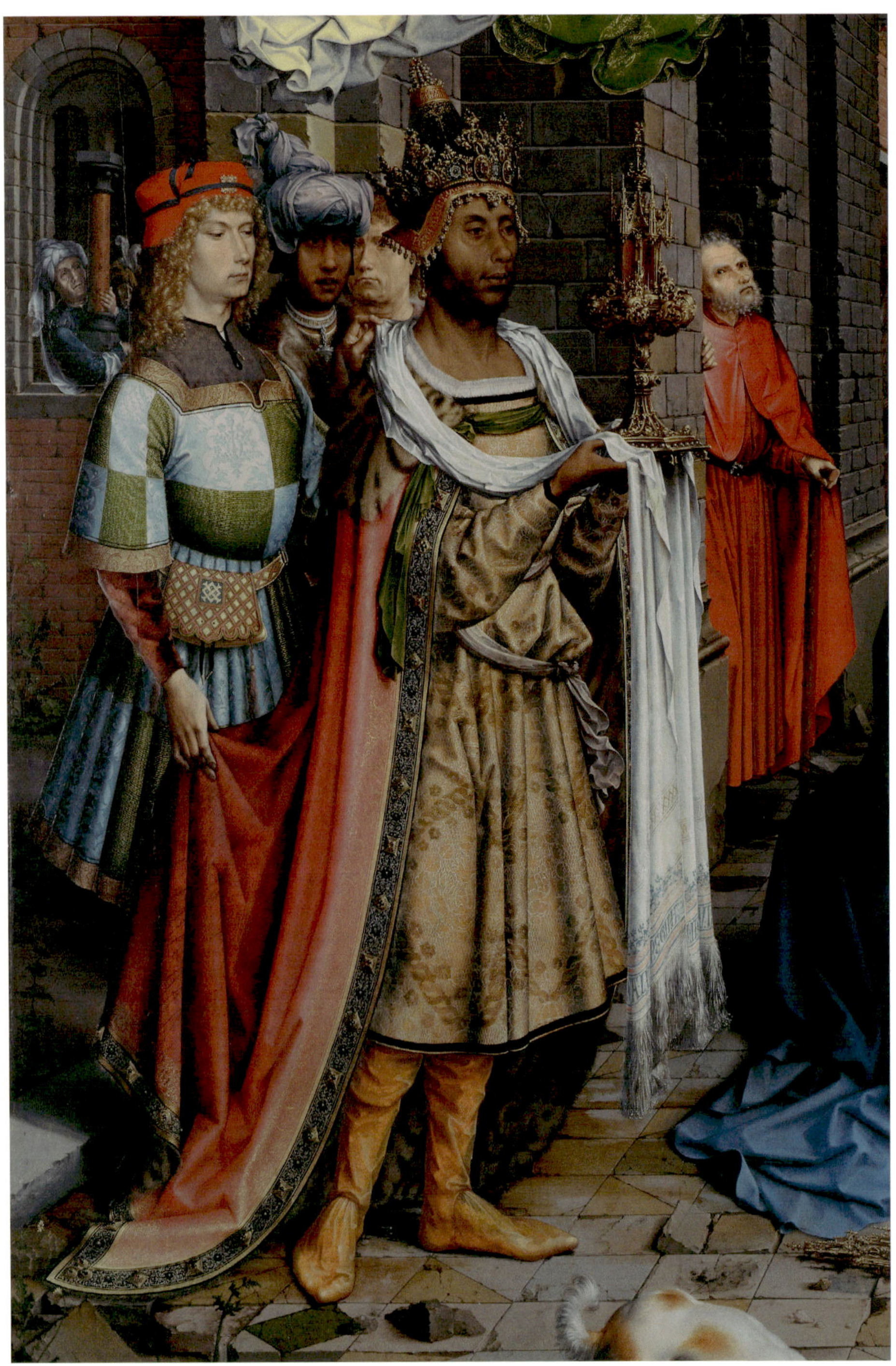

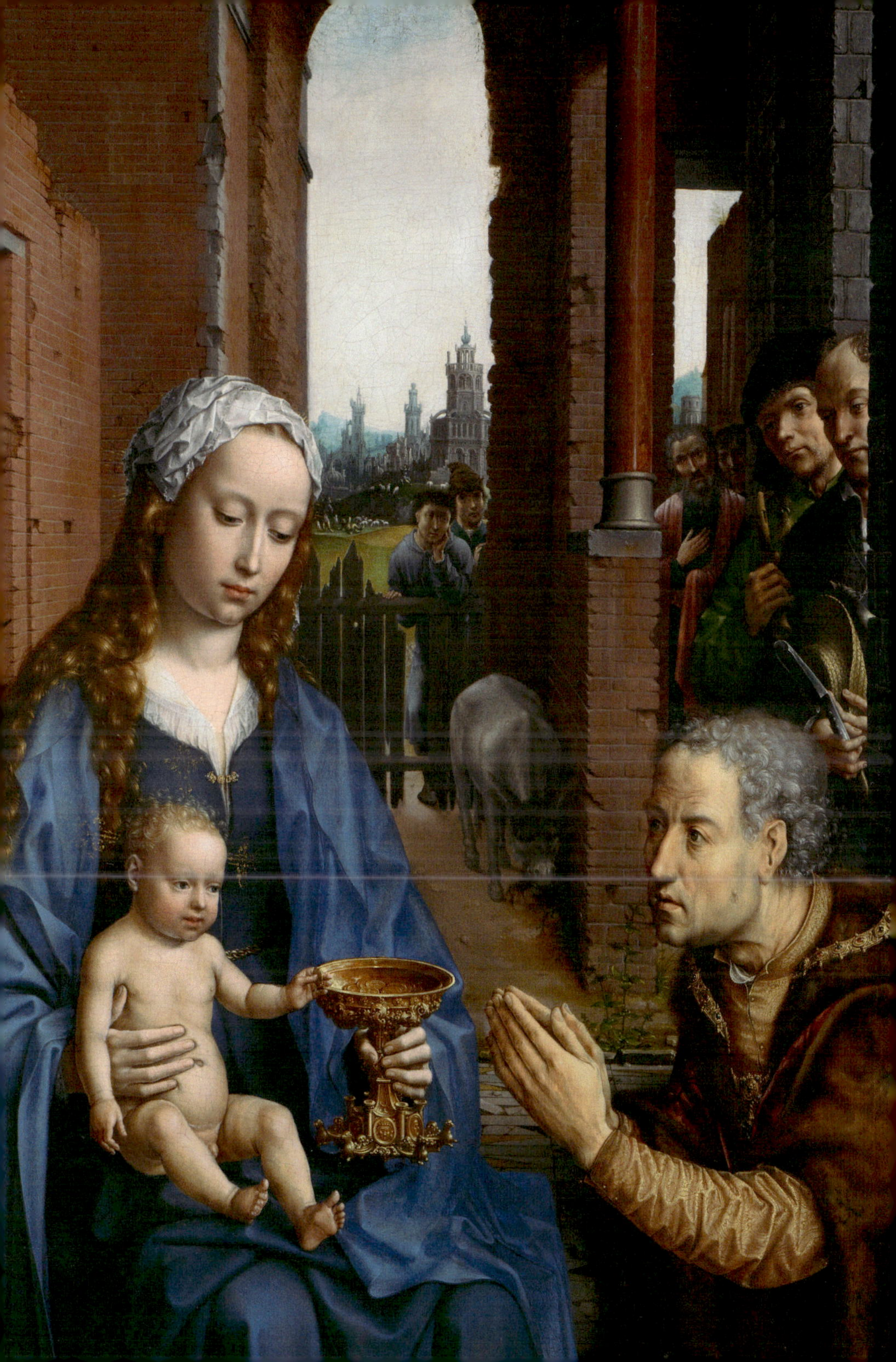

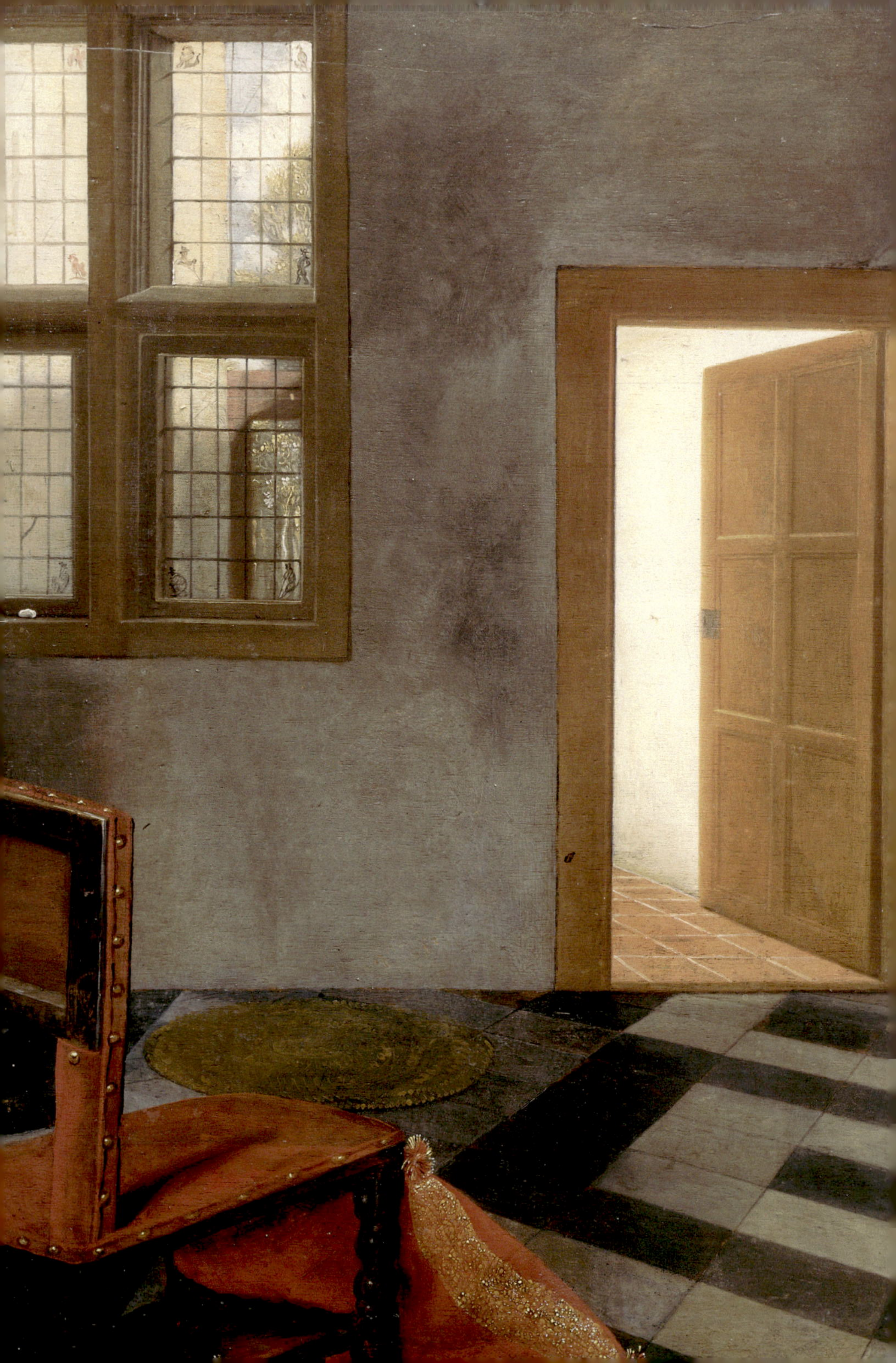

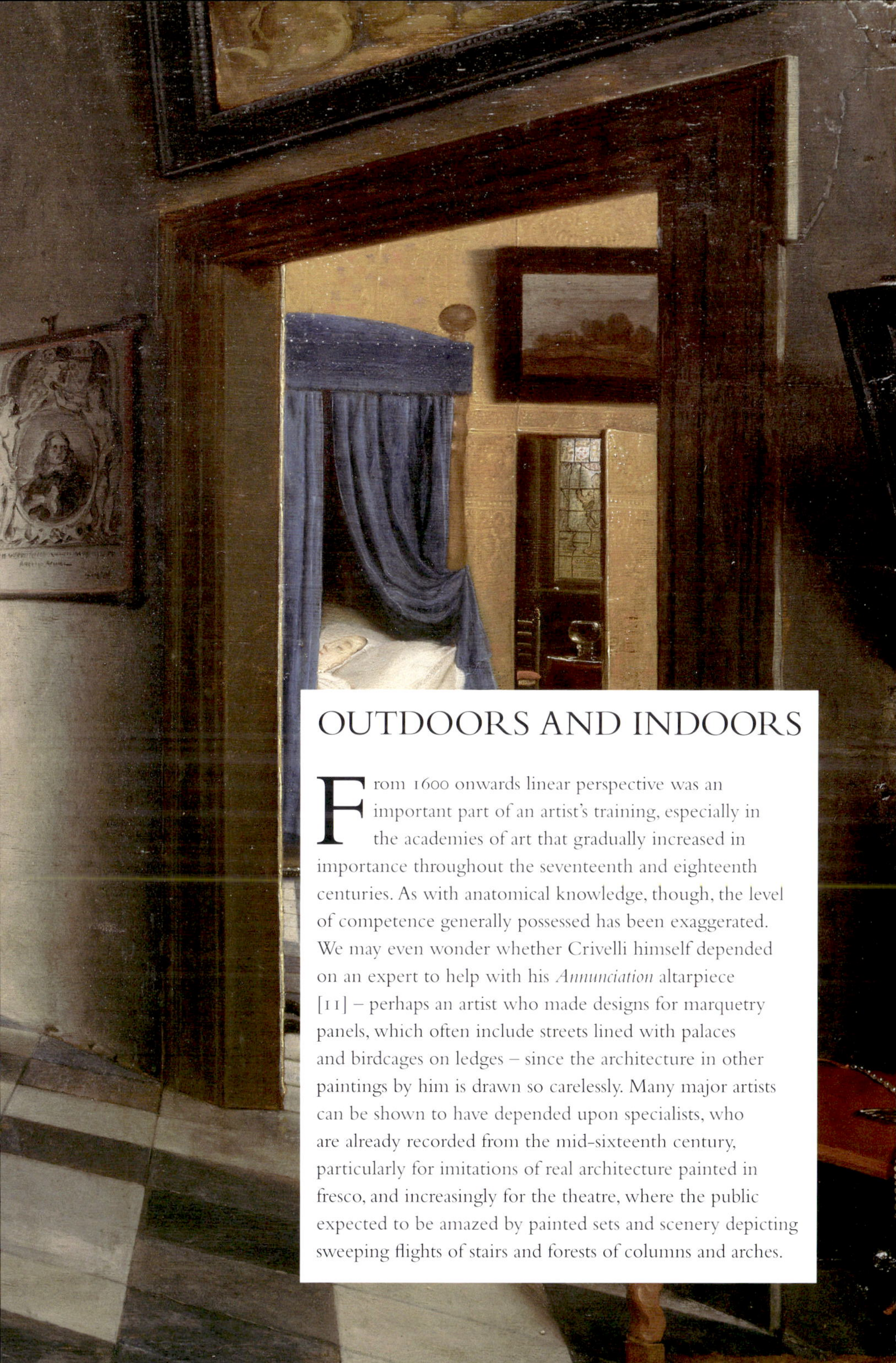

OUTDOORS AND INDOORS

From 1600 onwards linear perspective was an important part of an artist's training, especially in the academies of art that gradually increased in importance throughout the seventeenth and eighteenth centuries. As with anatomical knowledge, though, the level of competence generally possessed has been exaggerated. We may even wonder whether Crivelli himself depended on an expert to help with his *Annunciation* altarpiece [11] – perhaps an artist who made designs for marquetry panels, which often include streets lined with palaces and birdcages on ledges – since the architecture in other paintings by him is drawn so carelessly. Many major artists can be shown to have depended upon specialists, who are already recorded from the mid-sixteenth century, particularly for imitations of real architecture painted in fresco, and increasingly for the theatre, where the public expected to be amazed by painted sets and scenery depicting sweeping flights of stairs and forests of columns and arches.

A genre of easel painting emerged in the seventeenth century which reversed the priorities; in place of figure paintings with architectural settings supplied by an expert in *quadratura* (as linear perspective was known in Italy), we find architectural paintings animated by people, who were added by a secondary figurative artist.

Dirck van Delen's painting of palaces, loggia, terrace, triumphal arch and garden pavilion is a good example [15]. The size of the windows and pitched roofs suggest that this painting was made for a northern European patron and the types of coloured marble are characteristic of the Low Countries. Some of these buildings may have been imagined by the artist, or may at least have been projected in drawings seen by the painter. The gilded fountain in the foreground [16] is based on a print of one that was made for the city of Augsburg by Adriaen de Vries. Such paintings, which were made in all parts of Europe, are perfect in their way but lifeless, like the sterile computerised renderings produced by architects today to entice their clients. Time seems absent and the lighting is routine.

Painters of *vedute* (architectural views) enjoyed most prestige in the eighteenth century, and it is often forgotten that they employed their skill not only in topography (recording places) but in *capricci* (fanciful compositions), sometimes mixing actual buildings with projected ones (as van Delen may have done), sometimes inventing fantastic or ideal structures, or reconstructing ruins, and even depicting relatively recent constructions in a ruined state. Canaletto, the most famous of these artists, was as interested in making distortions seem plausible as he was in achieving accuracy in his renderings of familiar sites and festive spectacles. Some of his paintings might even be considered as advanced exercises in composition, where near and far are combined and shadows compete with solids in unexpected but compelling patterns.

A pair of small views of the Piazza San Marco [17, 18] provide a good example. They were probably intended to hang on opposite walls, for the shadows fall in different directions and the vanishing point is to the left of centre in one and right of centre in the other. In the first painting the tip of the campanile, the detached bell tower of the basilica of San Marco, crosses an iron bar that runs across the foreground arcade, and the thin line of sky between the campanile in the distance and the pillar in the foreground is especially thrilling. This, however, is less surprising than the way that, in the other painting, the foreground pillar, merged with a column behind

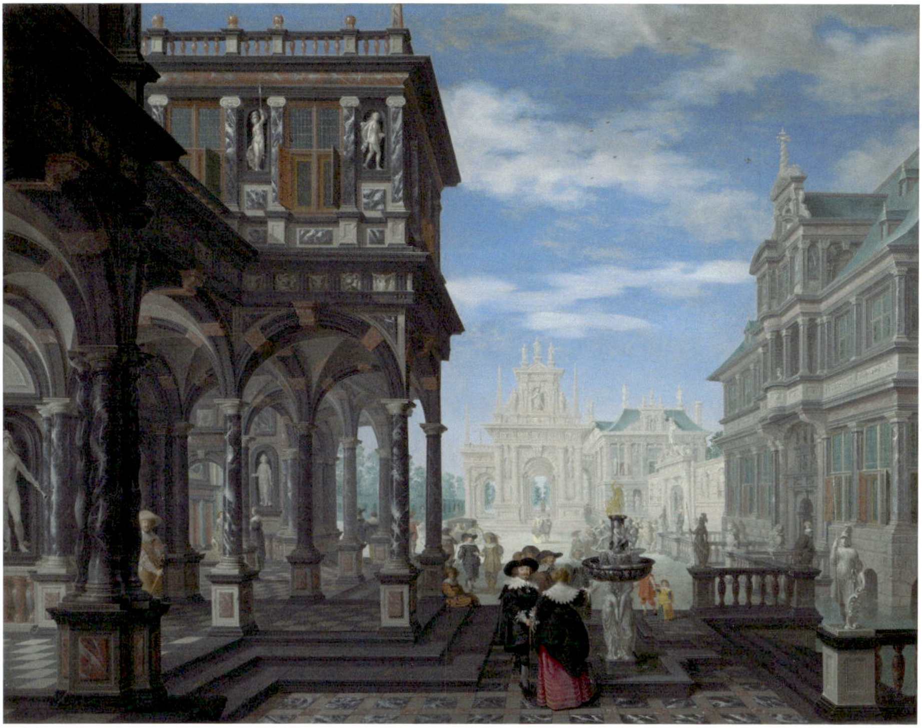

15. Dirck van Delen (with an
unknown figure painter),
An Architectural Fantasy, 1634.
The type of marble represented in
the columns on the left is the same
as that on the floor of Vermeer's
painting, fig. 23.

16. Detail from *An Architectural
Fantasy*. The fountain is based on
one by Adriaen de Vries which
was far larger.

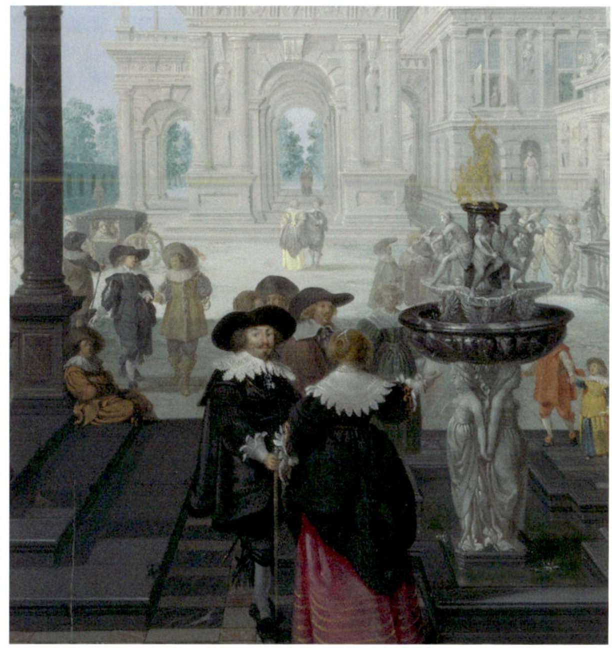

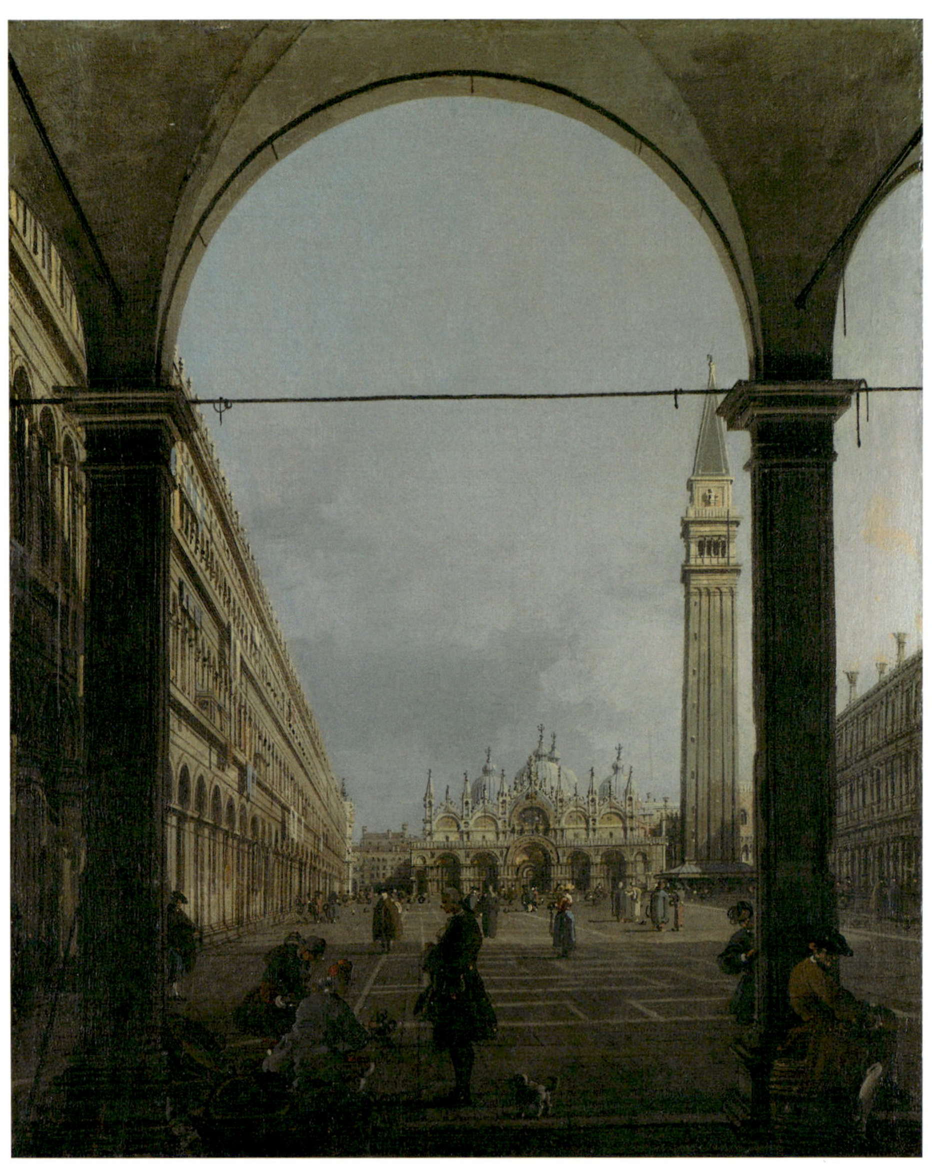

17. Canaletto, *Venice: Piazza San Marco*, about 1758.

it, is also combined with the campanile far beyond them both, a fine inverted stiletto of the shadowed side of the campanile separating them at the top and a blade of dark shadow slicing across the entablature. In common with other view painters, Canaletto made use of lenses that were devised to help with accurate drawing but which certainly also emphasised exciting but distorted features like these. It also

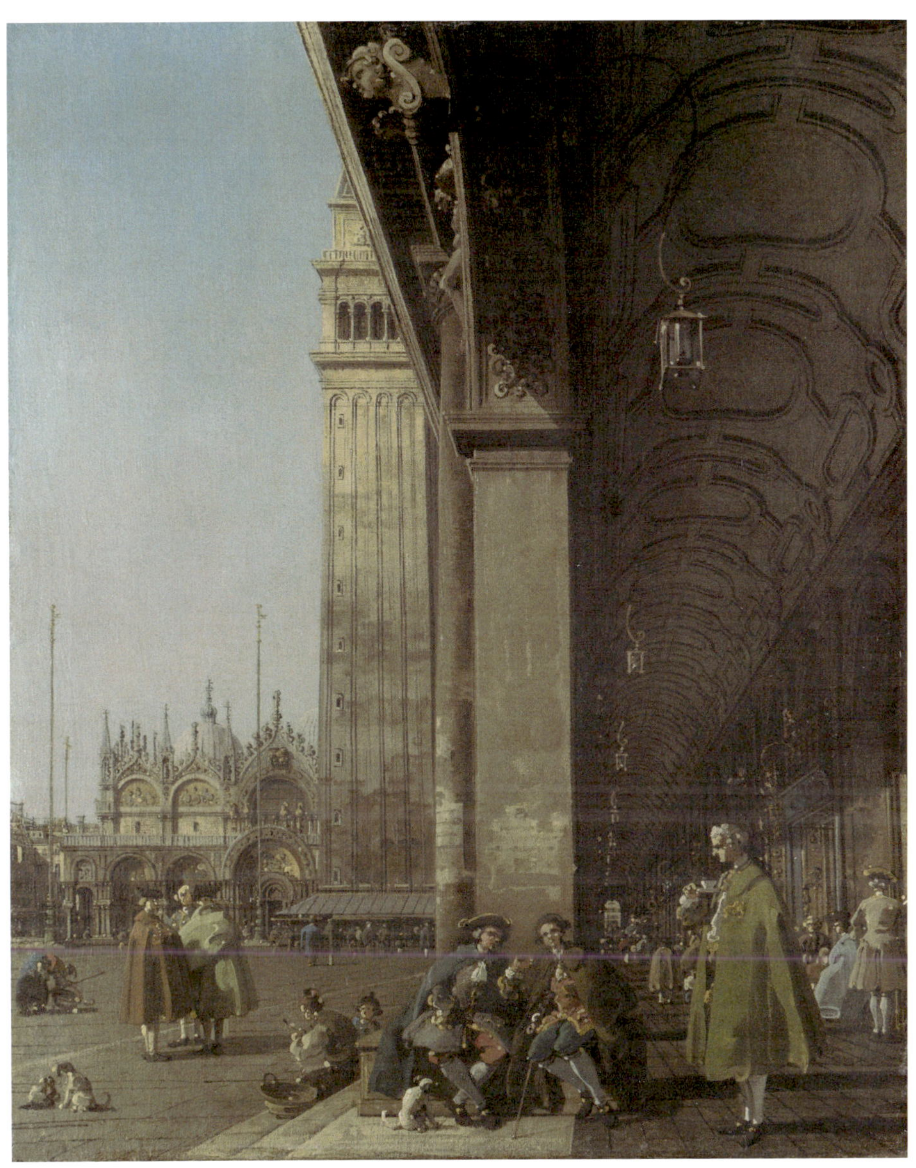

18. Canaletto, *Venice: Piazza San Marco and the Colonnade of the Procuratie Nuove*, about 1756.

seems possible that looking through lenses encouraged the development of a sort of punctuation that was employed for the representation of embellishments on buildings and on dress, and even for human beings and dogs – touches of creamy paint resembling commas and exclamation marks which, if we step back or half close our eyes, are recognisable as gentlemen conversing over coffee [19].

For the painting of interiors it is also true – perhaps even more obviously true – that the appeal of perspectival painting depends upon the representation of light. And light, because we know that it changes, brings with it a sense of time – the more precisely it is recorded the more we know that it will change. This can inject a sort of suspense into quiet and peaceful scenes. In the painting by Antonello da Messina [20] the stillness of Saint Jerome is enhanced by the great stone vaulted space around him. He is seated in a study no larger than a ship's cabin, set within a larger building, presumably an ecclesiastical palace (for this father of the Church was retrospectively endowed with the dignity of a cardinal). The silence is disturbed only by the soft footsteps of his tamed lion in the shadows on the right; by the distant splash of oars in the river, just discernible through the far window on the

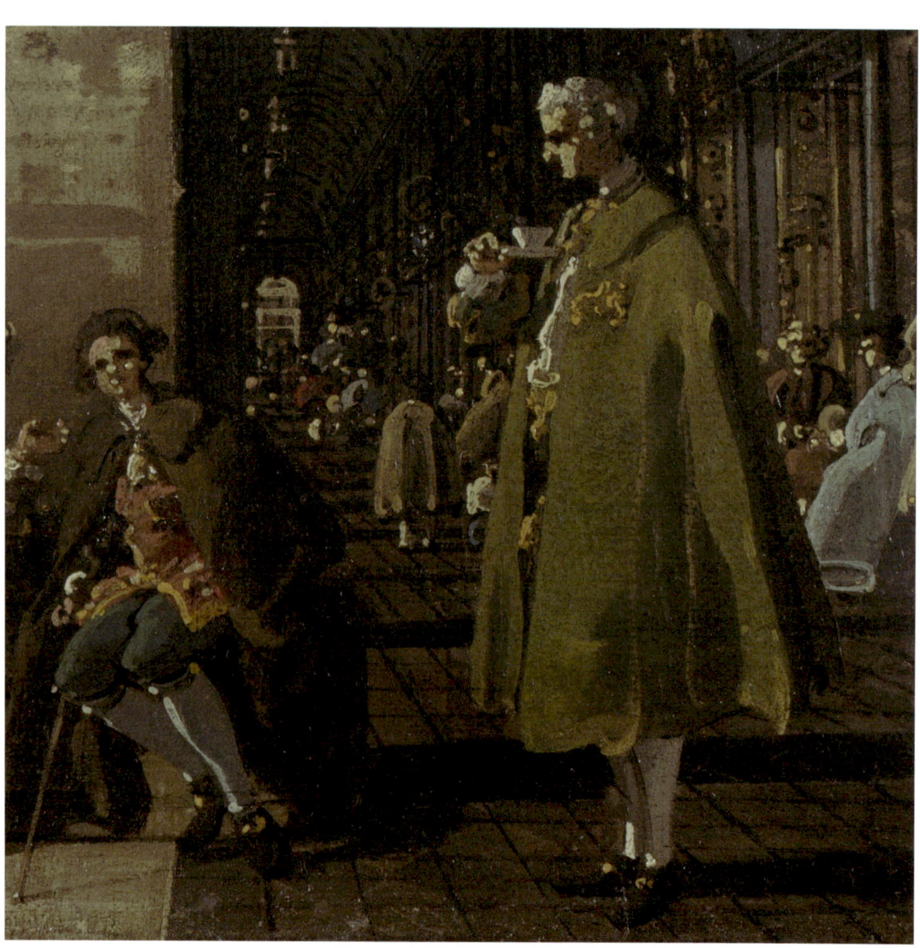

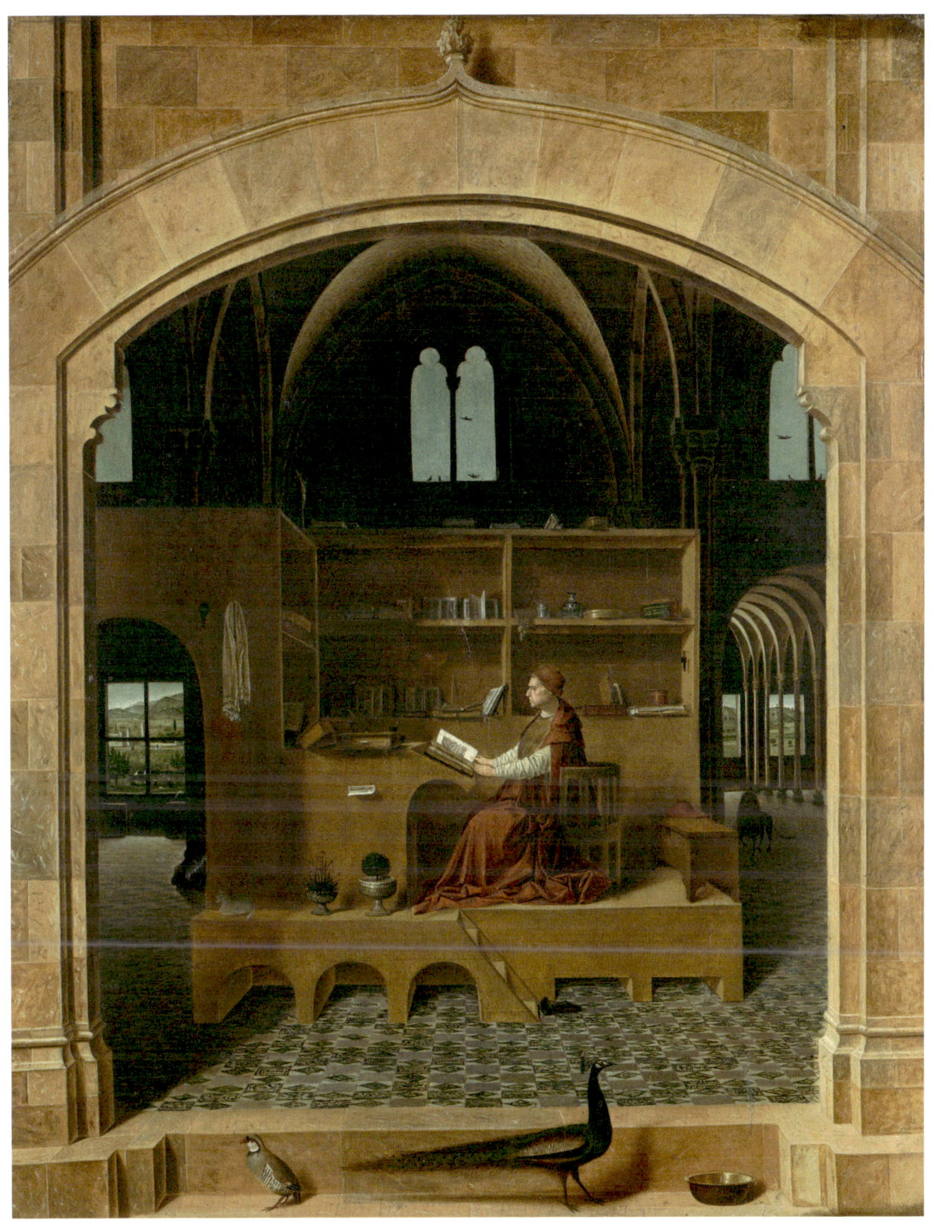

20. Antonello da Messina, *Saint Jerome
in his Study*, about 1475.

left; and soon, perhaps, by the slight movements of the partridge and peacock now stationary on the ledge in the foreground. The complex patterns of the floor tiles are legible only on those nearest to us and are otherwise concealed by shadow or by reflected light [see detail, page 92]. This means that the more visible receding lines also point towards the saint – a device that was later used by Gossaert [12]. The stone opening serves as a frame within the painting, dramatising the idea that we are somehow privileged intruders – a formula employed long afterwards by Gerrit Dou and Boilly, amongst others.

Opportunities for privacy increased in the seventeenth century, especially among a mercantile class whose status did not require a large retinue and the constant attendance of servants. Once established as precious, privacy was of course something that people wanted to invade. In Holland especially, private domestic rooms increased in importance. In these more silent, less populated homes surveillance was inevitably conducted by

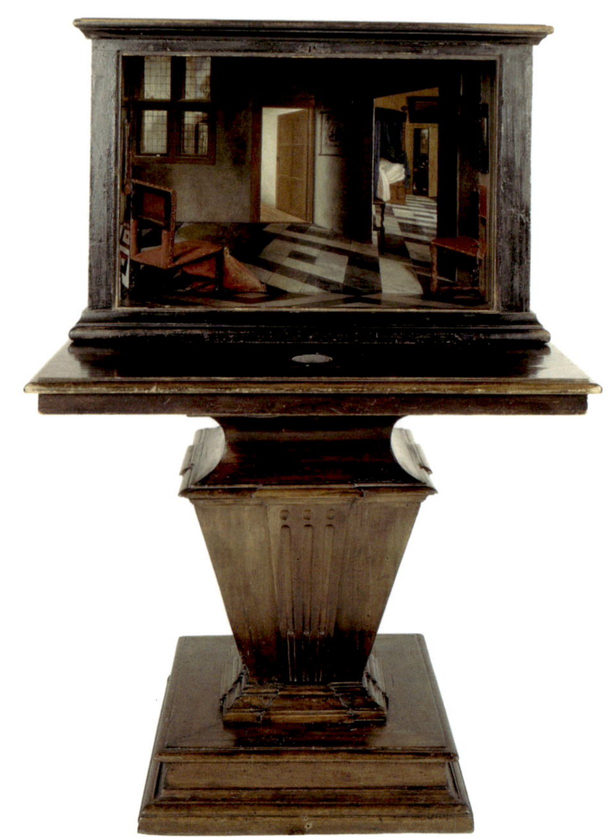

21. Samuel van Hoogstraten, *A Peep Show with Views of the Interior of a Dutch House*, about 1655–60. The peep show has two interior views (see pages 28–9 and opposite). Both views enable us to see how paintings were often placed over doors.

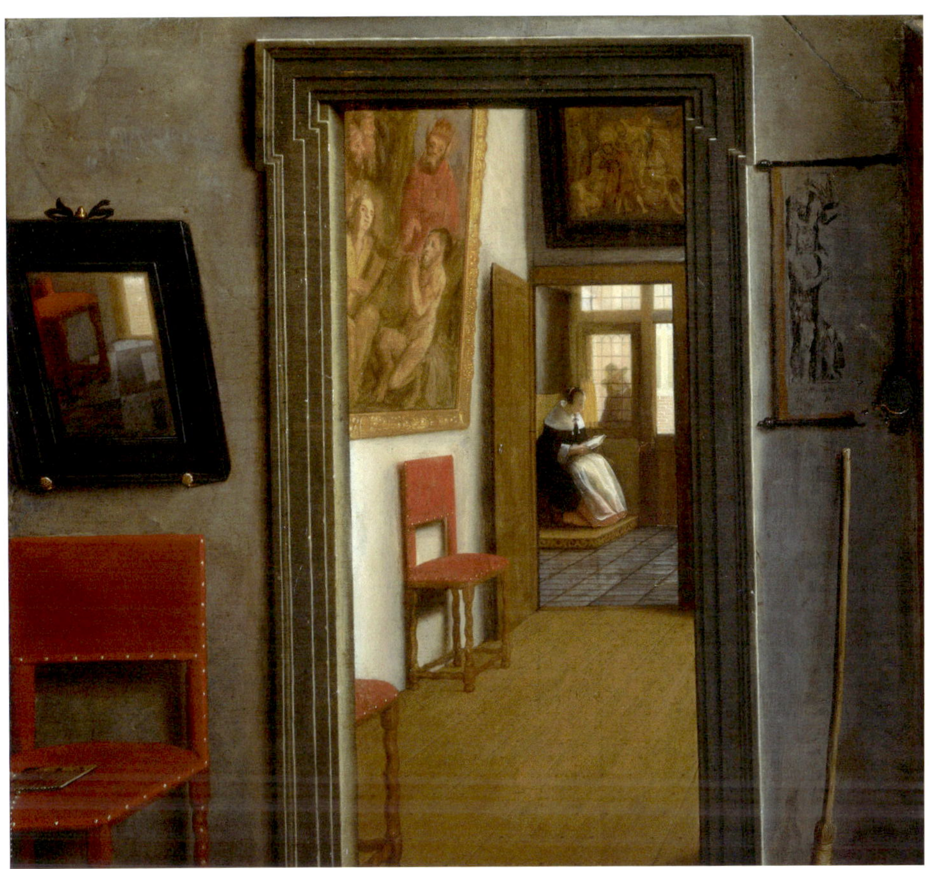

22. Detail from *A Peep Show with Views of the Interior of a Dutch House.*

all parties — and the painter enables us to spy on the daughter's music lesson, or on the carousing or slumbers of servants, or on the indiscreet chatter of a visitor in the parlour. Doll's houses that imitated the compartmentalised and intricate character of the modern house became popular. It was in Holland that the peep show was invented. Samuel van Hoogstraten's is one of the earliest, best preserved and most ambitious of these to have survived. It has two apertures permitting views of rooms giving on to rooms [21, 22].

Among the four or five great artists who painted the mundane but somehow mysterious activities that took place within such clean and genteel spaces, Jan Vermeer has now achieved a special fame. Like Canaletto at a later date, he probably took an interest in lenses (see page 32). He too turned legible forms into brilliant spots of light, although in his paintings it is not whole figures but rather the relief ornament on a carved and

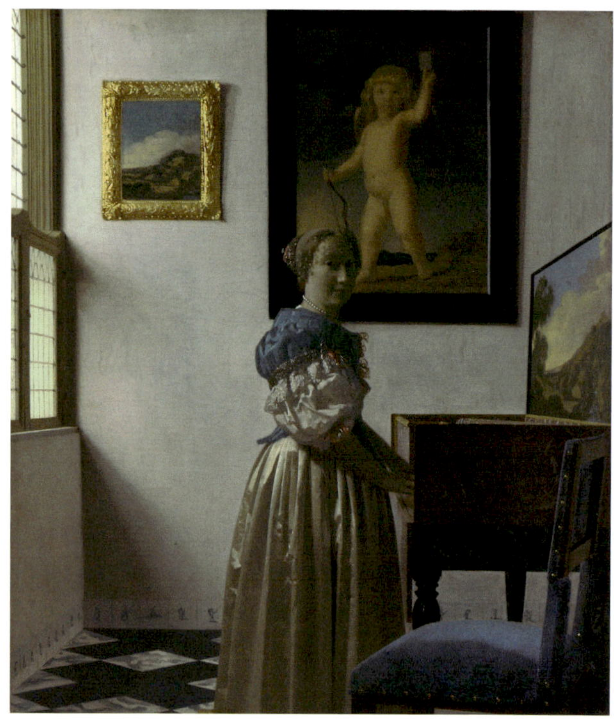

gilded picture frame, the lace and braid on a dress [24], or the crust on a loaf of bread that are dissolved in this way. In his *Young Woman standing at a Virginal* [23] the clear daylight casts double shadows, the blurred edges of which are recorded with breathtaking accuracy. But there is much that, seen through the lens of a camera, we would try to adjust or, found in a photograph, we might be inclined to edit. The chair is uncomfortably close to the painted landscape on the raised lid of the virginal, and the lid itself seems almost to touch the tilted black frame of the picture of Cupid hanging on the wall. Moreover, because the lid is cut by the edge of the painting, its shape is not certain (such lids were not always rectangles). There are three receding planes in the picture: the window and window wall, the virginal (including its drop front and raised lid), and the chair (especially the chair rail). Instead of making them work together Vermeer constructs an arrangement of geometric shapes with repetitions of black, blue and grey.

Interest in Vermeer's painting coincided with the recognition of photography as an art in the late nineteenth century; his reputation was further enhanced by the emergence of the more austere forms of abstract painting, such as the work of Mondrian.

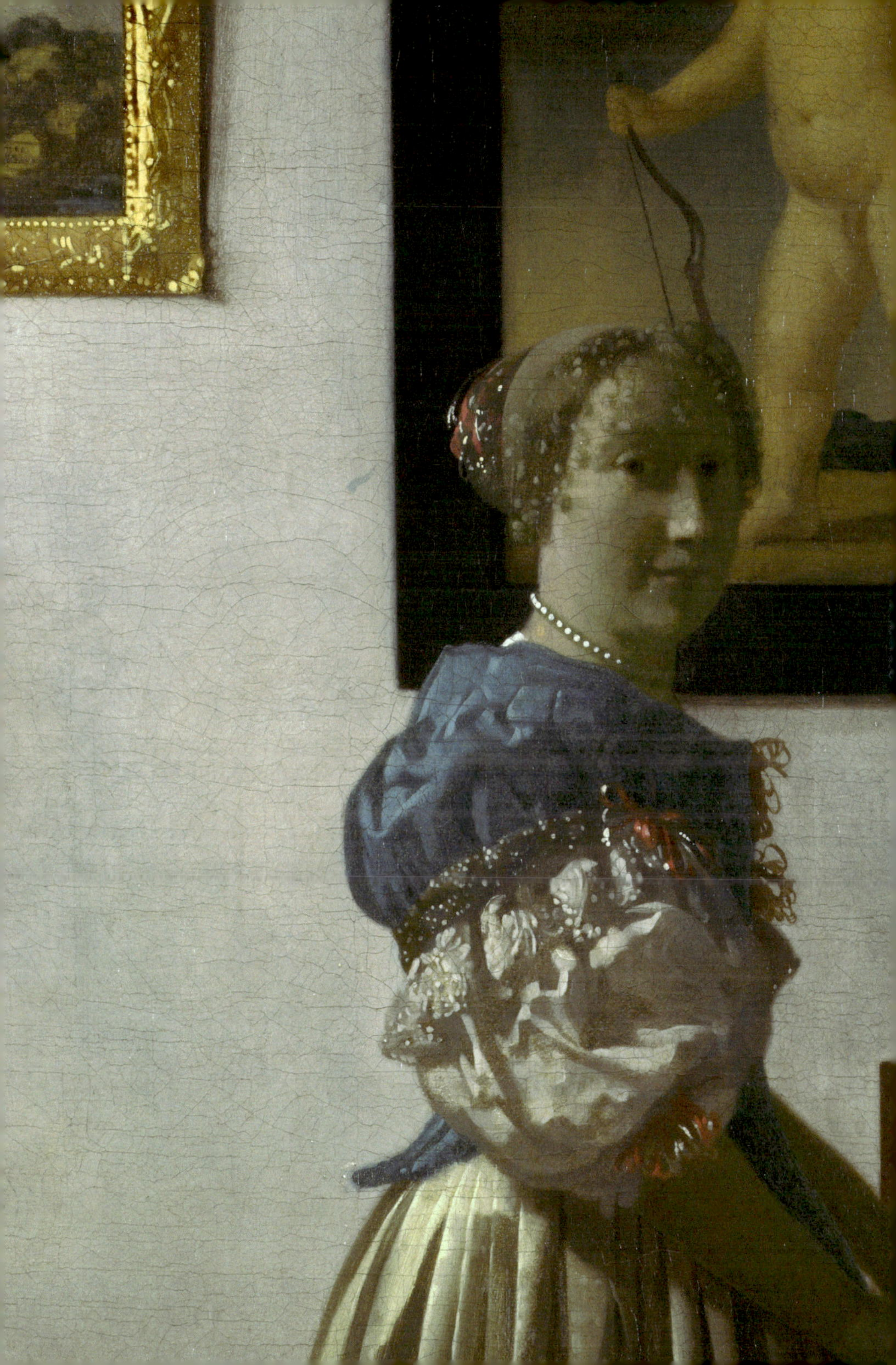

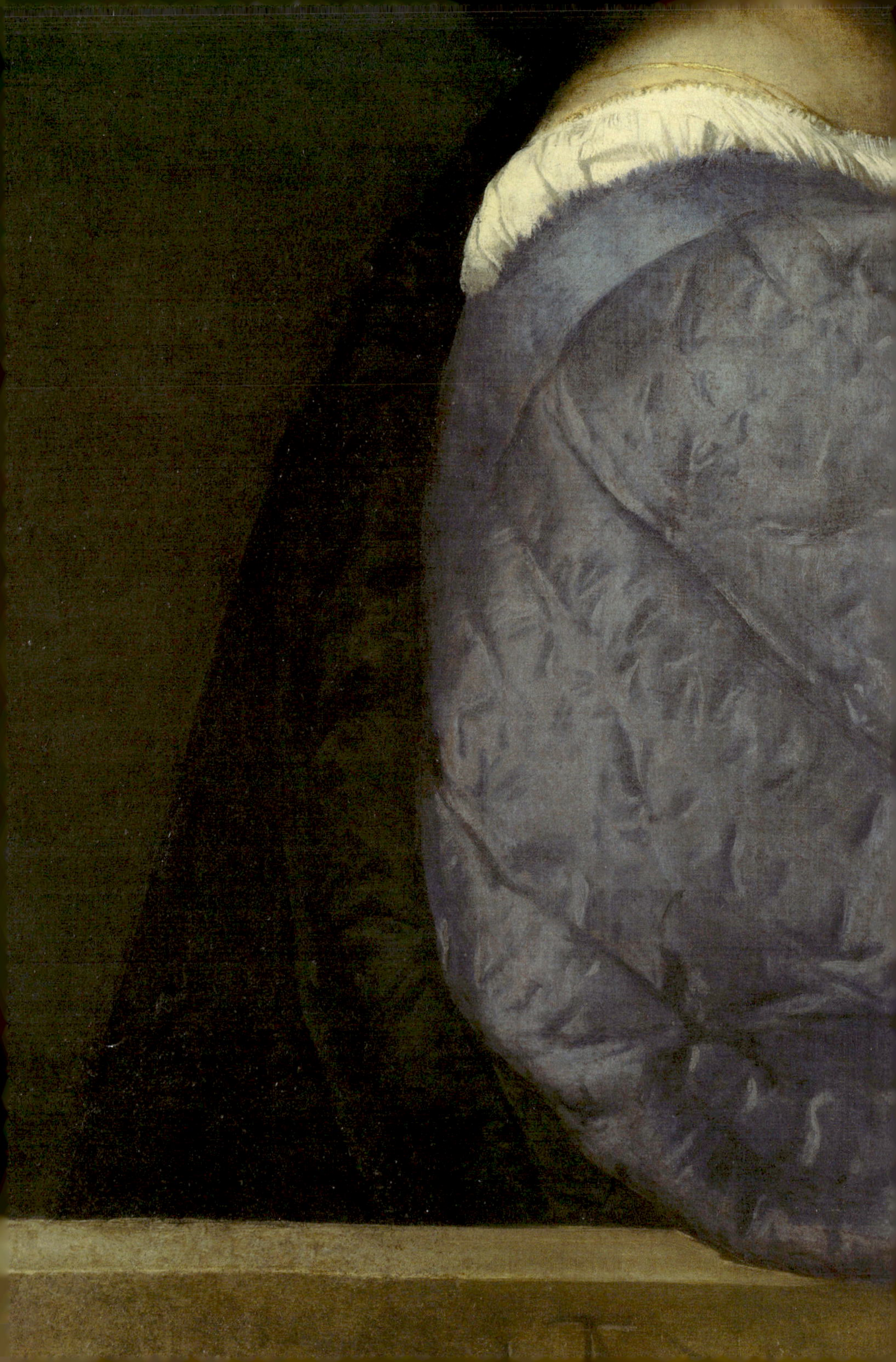

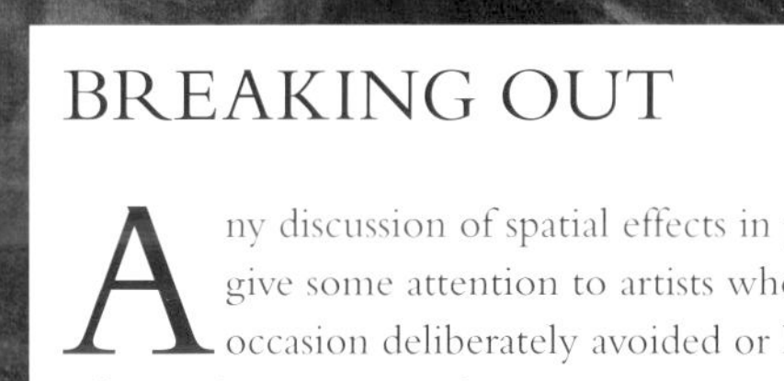

BREAKING OUT

Any discussion of spatial effects in painting should give some attention to artists who have on occasion deliberately avoided or limited such effects. This was true of Lorenzo Monaco and other artists throughout Europe who shared a liking for the flame-like rhythms of late Gothic tracery.

Later in the fifteenth century, German artists, despite creating three-dimensional figures, supplied hardly any space behind them. In the case of the *Deposition* by the Master of the Saint Bartholomew Altarpiece [25] the foreground is remarkably deep, with a special projection for the fainting Virgin Mary's spreading cloak (from beneath which the prehensile toes of Saint John make a surprise appearance) and for a little mound to display the ointment jar, the attribute that identifies Mary Magdalene. These elements project considerably from the foliate framing on three sides of the painting. The cross stands behind the figures but even the spider-like lad at the top of it seems to have broken through the pierced tracery crowning the frame [26].

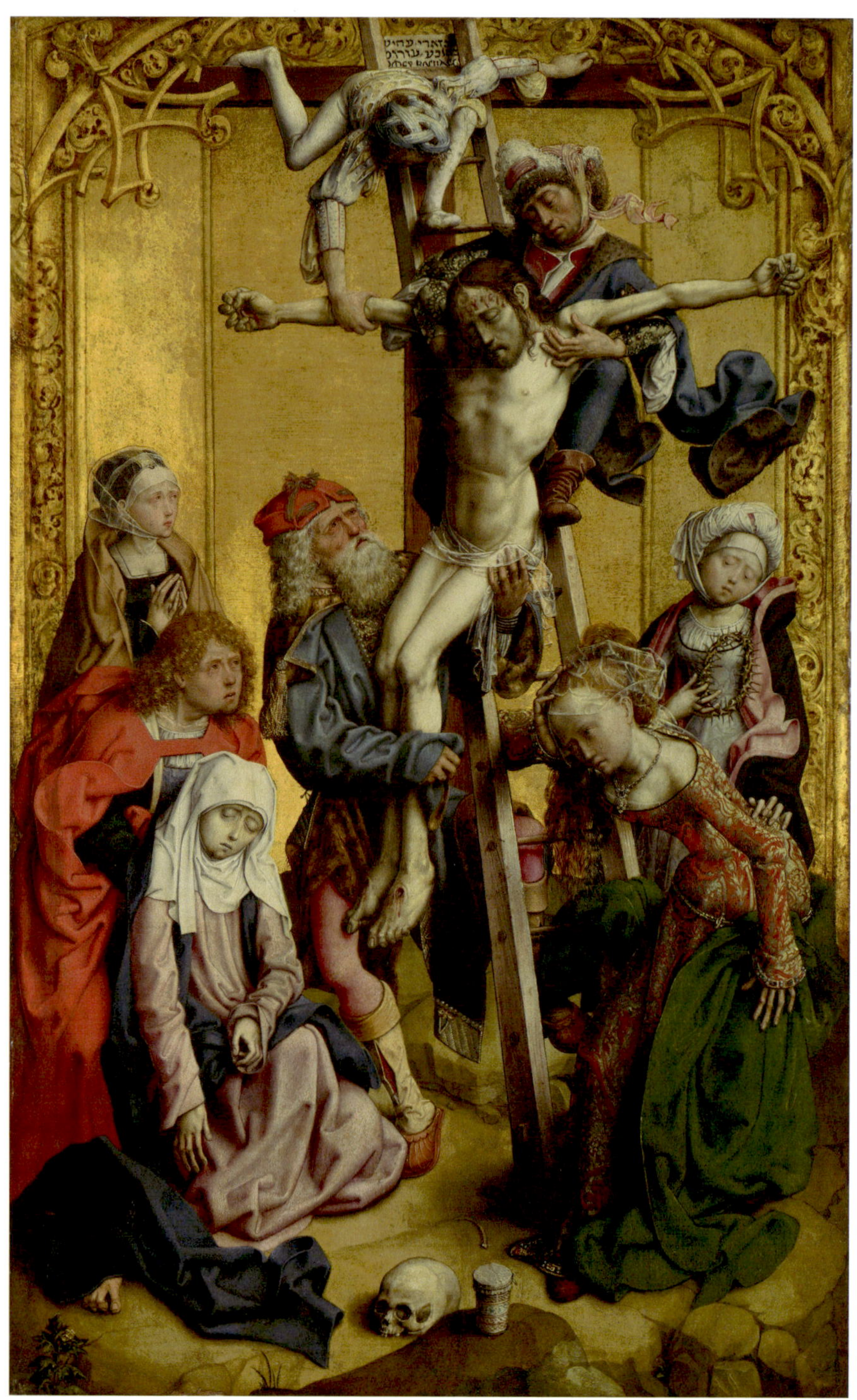

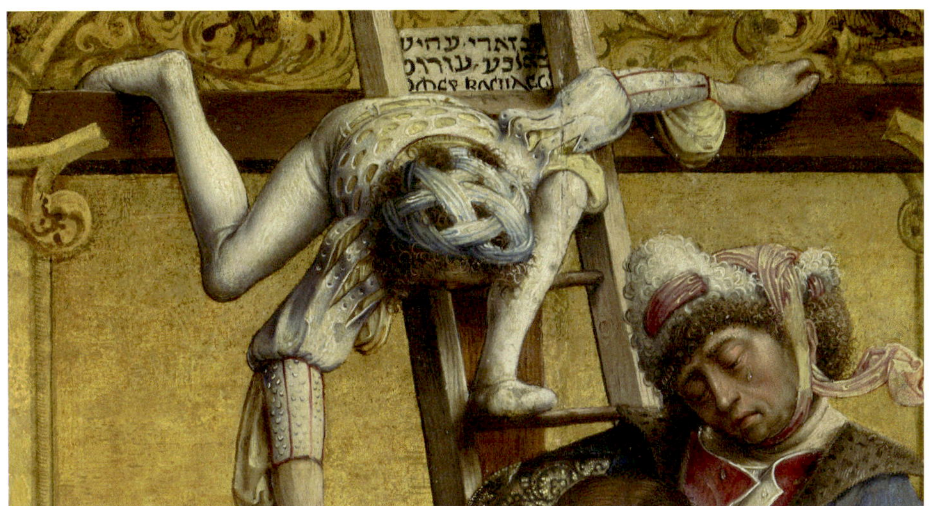

25. Master of the Saint Bartholomew Altarpiece, *The Deposition*, about 1500–5.

26. Detail from *The Deposition*. The acrobatic boy's toes and fingers are behind the bar of the cross. An arm and leg seem at first glance to have switched normal positions.

Previous pages: Titian, *Portrait of Gerolamo (?) Barbarigo*, about 1510, detail.

The figures occupy a gilded box with oblique side panels, exactly like those in high-relief wood carvings of that date. Indeed, the projecting features in the foreground are also typical of such carvings. Since the reliefs were built up out of carved planks arranged in layers, the relationship between the different planes was often awkward and the surprise appearance of a consoling hand on Mary Magdalene's back imitates perfectly the sort of effect often found in these carvings when one layer joins another.

In much of Europe during the fifteenth century, sculpture was painted – often completely – although when made of ivory, white alabaster or gold these precious materials were revealed. Painters were intimately familiar with sculpture because they often had the job of painting and decorating it. But why even the very greatest among them so frequently imitated such sculpture is not obvious. It may have been as a sort of witty competition, although the obvious competitive strategy would have been to depict the aerial perspective that was beyond the power of sculpture. More important may have been a desire to match the appearance of the sculpture in the many large and complex altarpieces in which paintings and sculpture were conjoined. In addition, painters may have wanted to concentrate the viewer's attention on the foreground action. Breaking into 'our' space may have seemed more important than leading us into the distance.

A parallel imitation of sculpture may be found in the work produced by Andrea Mantegna in north-east Italy. *The Introduction*

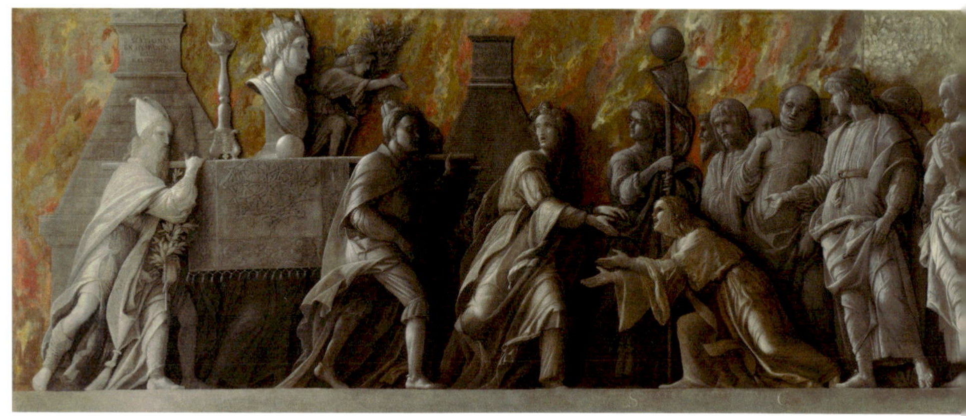

of the Cult of Cybele at Rome, one of his last works, was a fictive sculptural frieze for a palace of the Cornaro family in Venice [27]. Although the representation of distant landscape and receding architecture had become a major preoccupation of Italian sculptors during the fifteenth century (especially in Florence), it was not found in the marble reliefs or the miniature cameos of the ancient world that Mantegna wished to evoke, and he avoided the use of such devices in this painting. In place of a background, he has imitated a veneer of two pieces of patterned marble or alabaster (the division between them seems to indicate a point where he has compressed the narrative). He was, however, aware of the way such stone, with its streaked and cloudy pattern and its translucency, can even suggest the sky at sunset or sunrise.

As this painting is a frieze, intended to be placed high up in a room, the vanishing point on which receding lines would converge is well below the feet of the figures. Such lines are only apparent on the steps to the right of the composition [28] but we do notice that the feet of the two, or possibly even three, bearers of the litter that supports the bust of the goddess are not fully visible. The figures are shown moving and turning with much variety (although, oddly, the second and fifth heads from the right seem to be identical in features and expression) and they overlap, so that at several points they are three deep. There is none of the emphasis on clarity of outline and eloquent interval that would make a frieze more legible, and it is not easy to believe that much of the refinement of facial expression and exquisite detail in the drapery could easily have been appreciated when the painting was displayed in its original position.

There are other paintings in the National Gallery that were

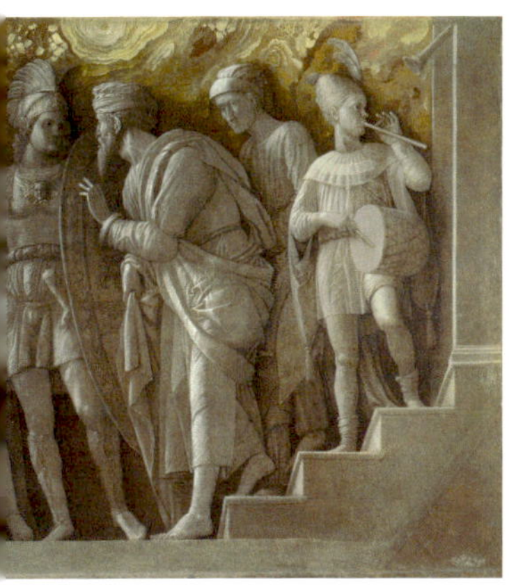

27. Andrea Mantegna, *The Introduction of the Cult of Cybele at Rome*, 1505–6.

28. Detail from *The Introduction of the Cult of Cybele at Rome*. The triangle of canvas in the lower right corner is not original. It seems possible that the hood of a chimney interrupted the frieze of the room for which this was painted.

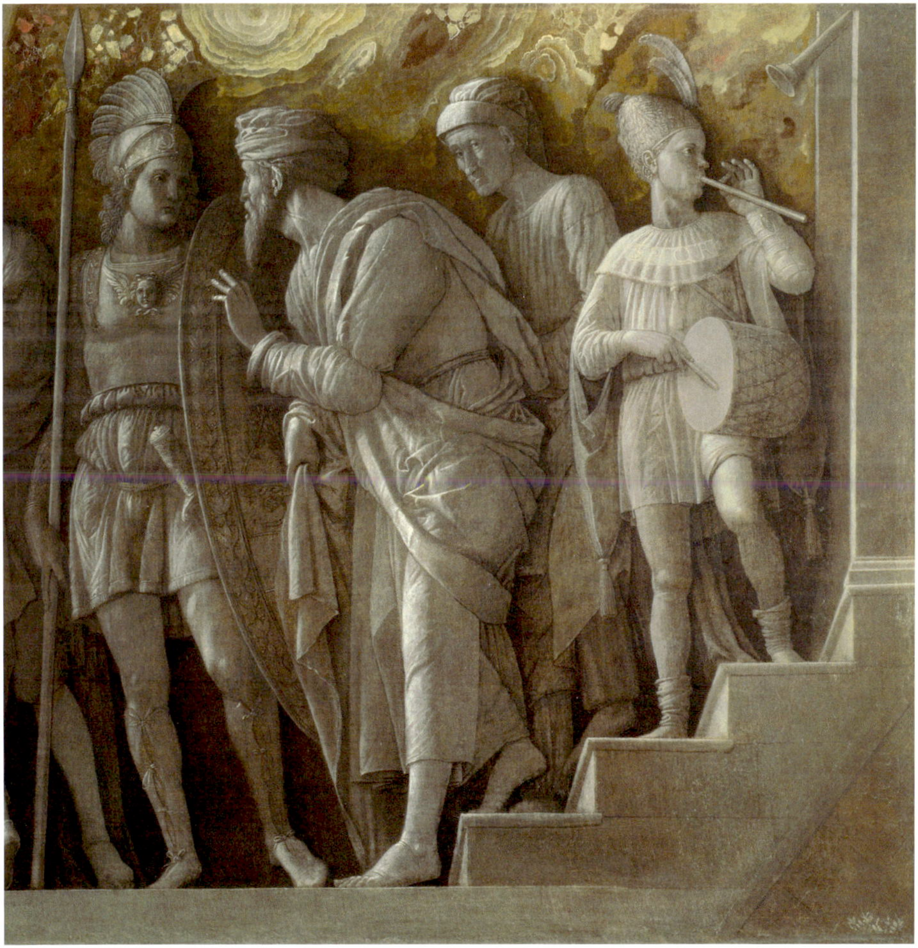

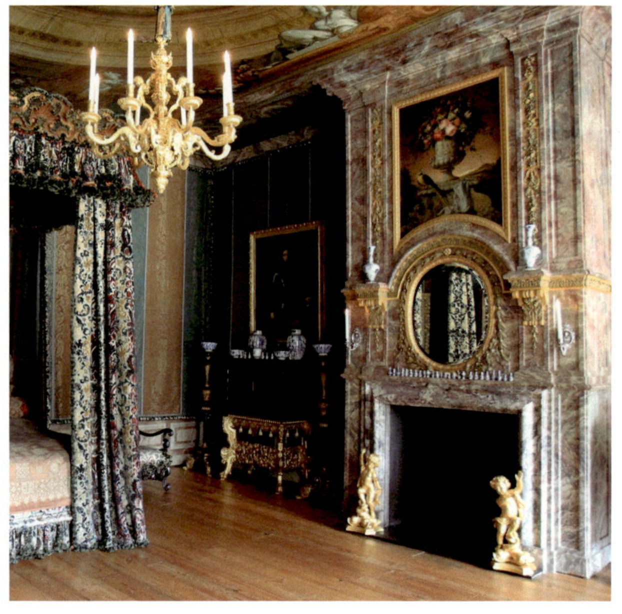

29. The Queen's closet at Het Loo Palace, Apeldoorn. The arrangement of a painting over a mirror was popular in eighteenth-century Holland. Jan van Huysum's flower piece may have been displayed in such a location, or above a door.

30 and 31 (detail, overleaf). Jan van Huysum, *Flowers in a Terracotta Vase*, 1736–7.

originally made to be displayed high up in a room, most commonly above a tall chimney ('overmantle') or above a door. Between about 1600 and 1850 grand rooms not otherwise designed to incorporate paintings would frequently be supplied with overmantles and overdoors. Subjects deemed suitable for an overdoor, especially when a set of four was required, were the seasons, the elements, personifications of the arts, or the ages of man, but landscapes, portraits (even full-length portraits) and flower pieces were also employed. Real flowers could never have been conveniently displayed in such an elevated position and this may have made it especially appealing to see painted still lifes there. In Holland paintings were often placed over a mirror which was set above a chimney [29]. In one of the flower pieces by van Huysum in the National Gallery [30], the apparent tilting of the marble plinth for the terracotta vase – clearly in anticipation of the low viewing-point – suggests that it was originally in one of these high positions.

When a painting was set above the door, the door frame (in many cases crowned not only by a projecting entablature but also by a segmental or triangular pediment) would have obscured part of it from most vantage points. The same might be true of the frame of a mirror beneath the painting. In the case of van Huysum's flower piece we may conjecture that, once it had been put in place, the artist or his patron proposed that a dangling

46

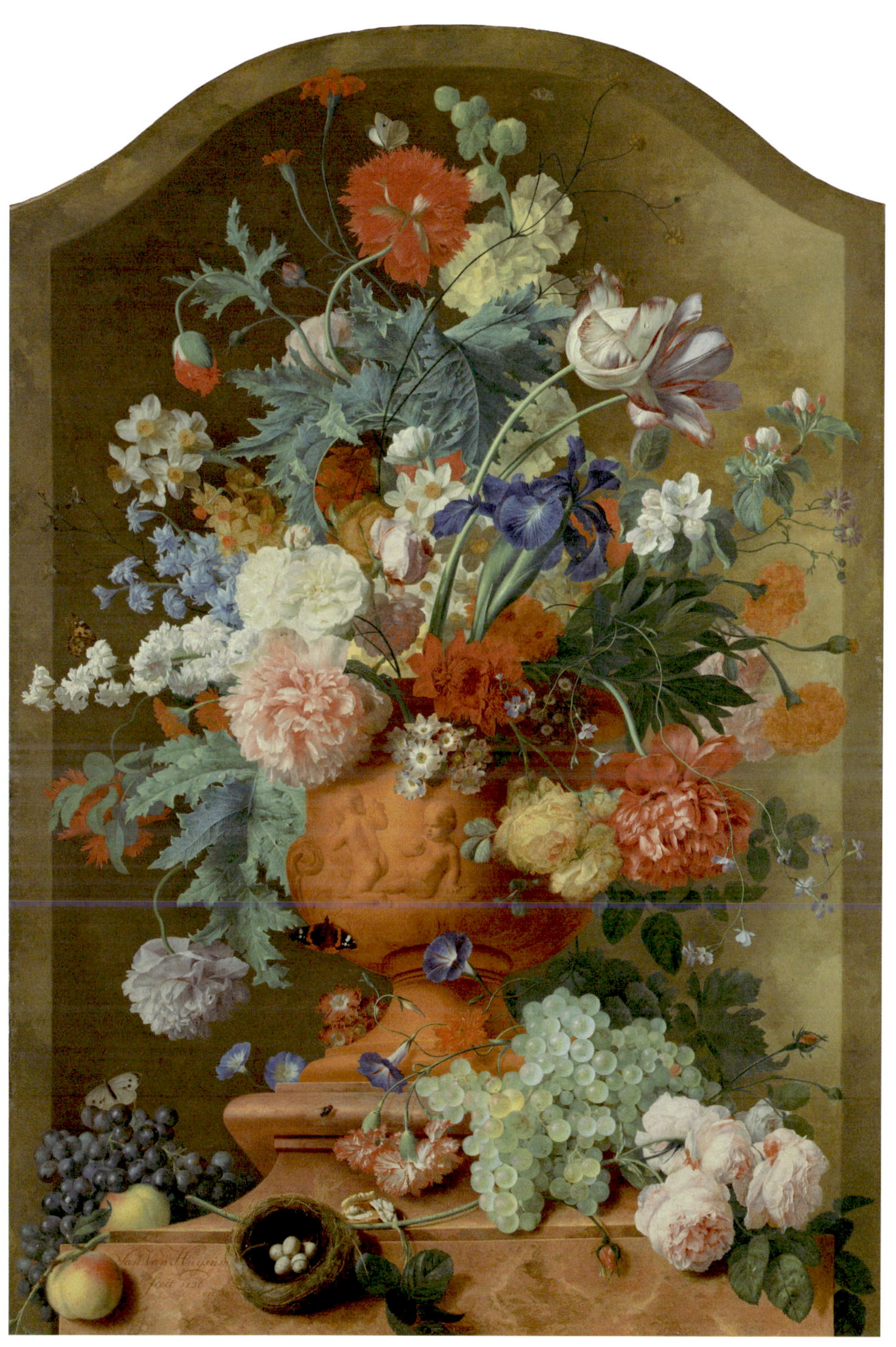

Jan Van Huijsum
fecit 1736
en

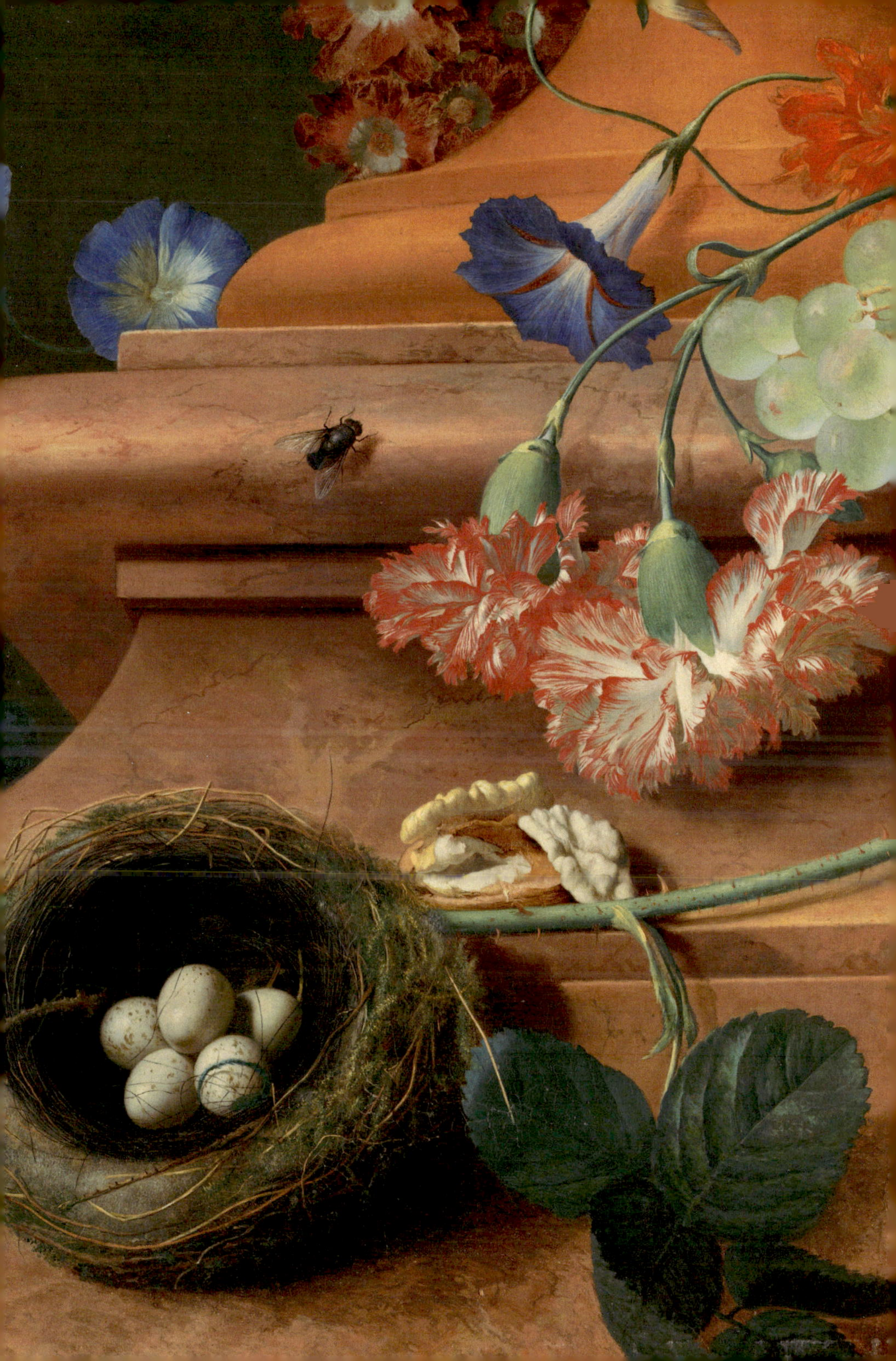

peach and a bird's nest be added to the very front of the composition to make it look as if they were resting against the entablature or mirror frame. Having added these, van Huysum must have dated the painting a second time [31] – this in fact is the only reasonable explanation for the two dates. Once the painting had been removed from its original setting, the nest looked absurd, as if it were floating on air, and the peach seemed to be inadequately supported. What remains puzzling, as with Mantegna's frieze, is the amount of detail that could never have been fully appreciated from any distance. Indeed, the bluebottle on the uppermost moulding of the marble plinth and the smallest of the thirty-odd flowers in this spectacular arrangement (the honesty overlapping the edge to the right) would hardly have been visible.

Van Huysum's peach and bird's nest almost qualify as *trompe l'oeil*. The occasions on which the eye is ever actually deceived by a painting are very rare, although a fly in an oil painting, carefully rendered together with its shadow, can often be mistaken for a real one on its surface; and in fresco decorations of fictive architecture, when viewed in the natural light for which they were planned, distant mouldings or even pilasters can also be mistaken for real ones. But a form of half-deception – the equivalent in painting of the 'willing suspension of disbelief' that Coleridge defined in his discussion of our experience in the theatre – is common enough, especially when the objects represented are the size of life. Moreover, a preparedness to be deceived was surely stronger in former centuries when it was not considered to be a naive or uneducated attitude, as tends to be the case today.

Crivelli in his *Annunciation* [11] seeks not only to draw us into the fictive space of his painting but to break into our space; the cucumber resting on the foreground ledge or plinth is a case in point [34]. This device was an important characteristic of the school of still-life painting that flourished in Spain during the seventeenth and eighteenth centuries. Luis Meléndez was especially fond of including at least one object that projects over a shelf parallel to the front plane of the picture. The space in his paintings is relatively shallow but the objects, which always strike us as life-size, press forward into our own space – or almost into our hands in the case of the lemons and oranges in one of Meléndez's paintings in the National Gallery [32]. They seem to be pushed from behind by the contiguous convex volumes of a jar, a watermelon, a bottle and a basket. It would be interesting to discover how such paintings as this were originally displayed.

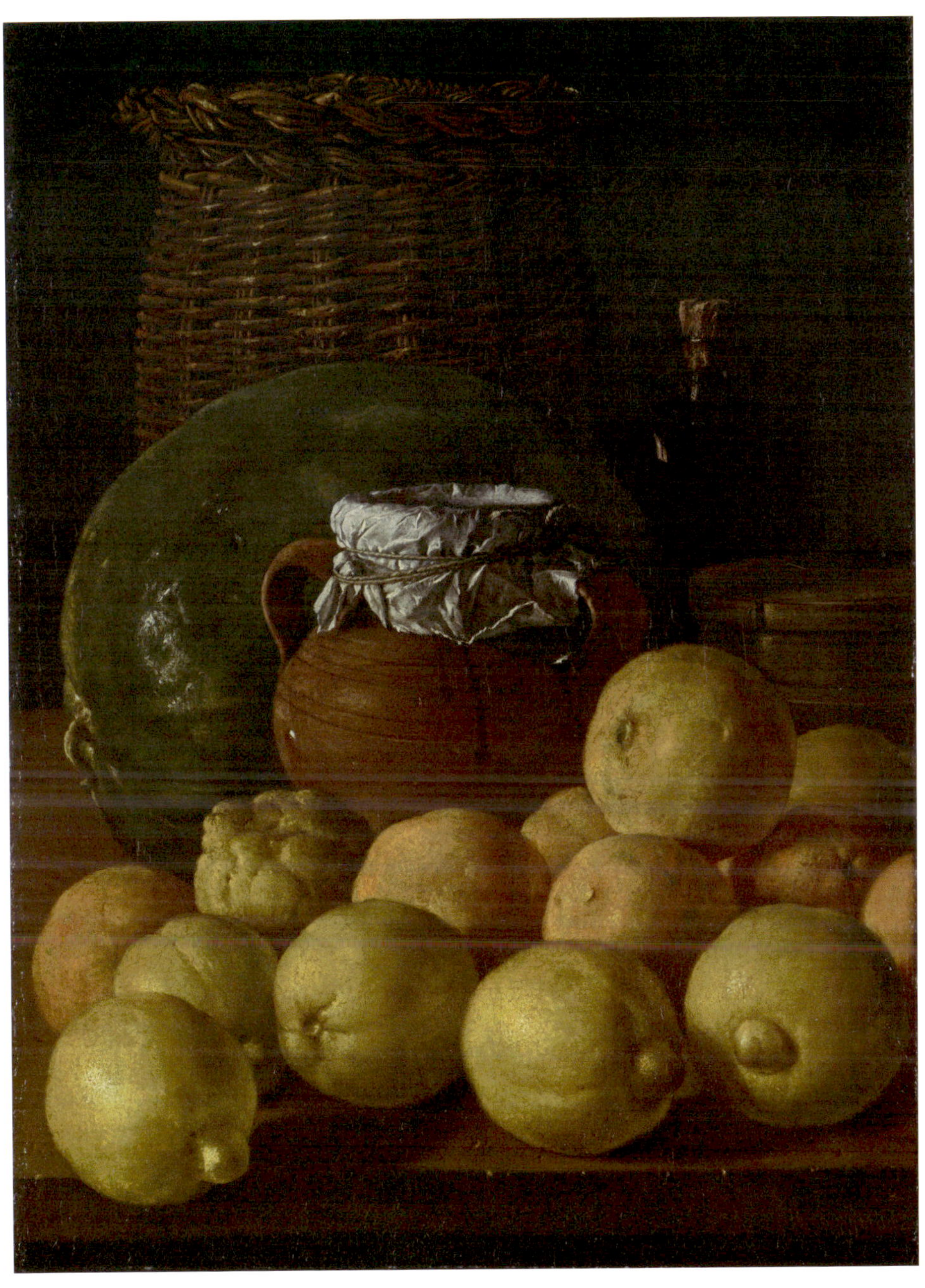

32. Luis Meléndez, *Still Life with Lemons and Oranges*, 1760s.

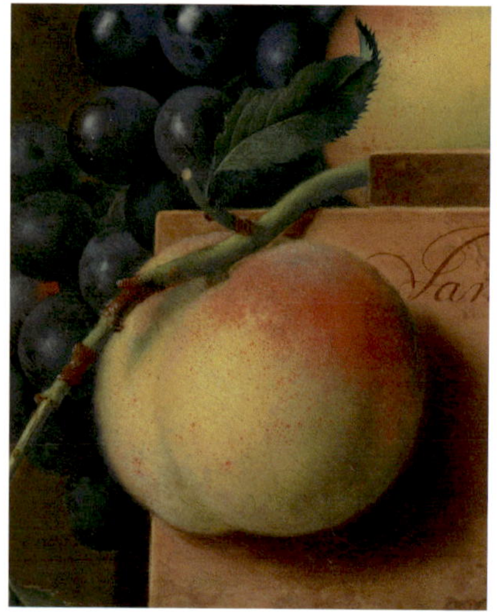 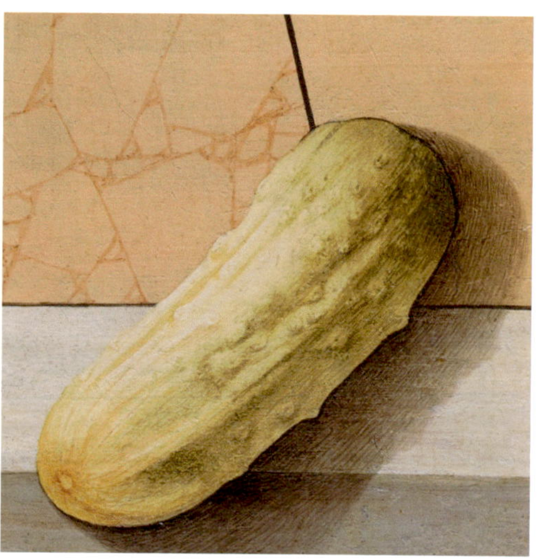

33. Detail from *Flowers in a Terracotta Vase* (see fig. 30).

34. Detail from *The Annunciation, with Saint Emidius* (see fig. 11).

At the right level, in the relatively dim light of domestic interiors in a hot climate before the advent of ubiquitous electric lighting, their impact would have been far greater than can easily be imagined in an artificially lit public gallery.

Crivelli's cucumber was painted long before the fruit added by van Huysum to his *Flowers in a Terracotta Vase* [30, 33]. Many other examples of the 'foreground breakthrough', as it might be called, can be found in fifteenth-century paintings made in different parts of Europe: for example, tails of drapery or fingers painted over the frames of portraits or devotional images when these were continuous with the painted support. They hardly prepare us for the extraordinary impact in the early sixteenth century of Titian's portrait of a member of the Barbarigo family, long known as *The Man with a Quilted Sleeve* because that salient feature seems to swell out of the painting into the space of the beholder [35]. In addition, the sitter seems, albeit silently, to respond to the viewer's presence. Many portraits after 1500 in Europe were made for particular places, and the lighting in the painting would have been adjusted to match the direction from which light entered the room where it was intended to hang. The background here, uniform in colour, recedes, suggesting an airy but unspecified space around the sitter. This device would be imitated in many later portraits, including those by Velázquez, and it is also found in a great portrait of a horse.

The Marquess of Rockingham's racehorse Whistlejacket, painted by George Stubbs, is the most remarkable example in the National Gallery of a painting in which colour alone

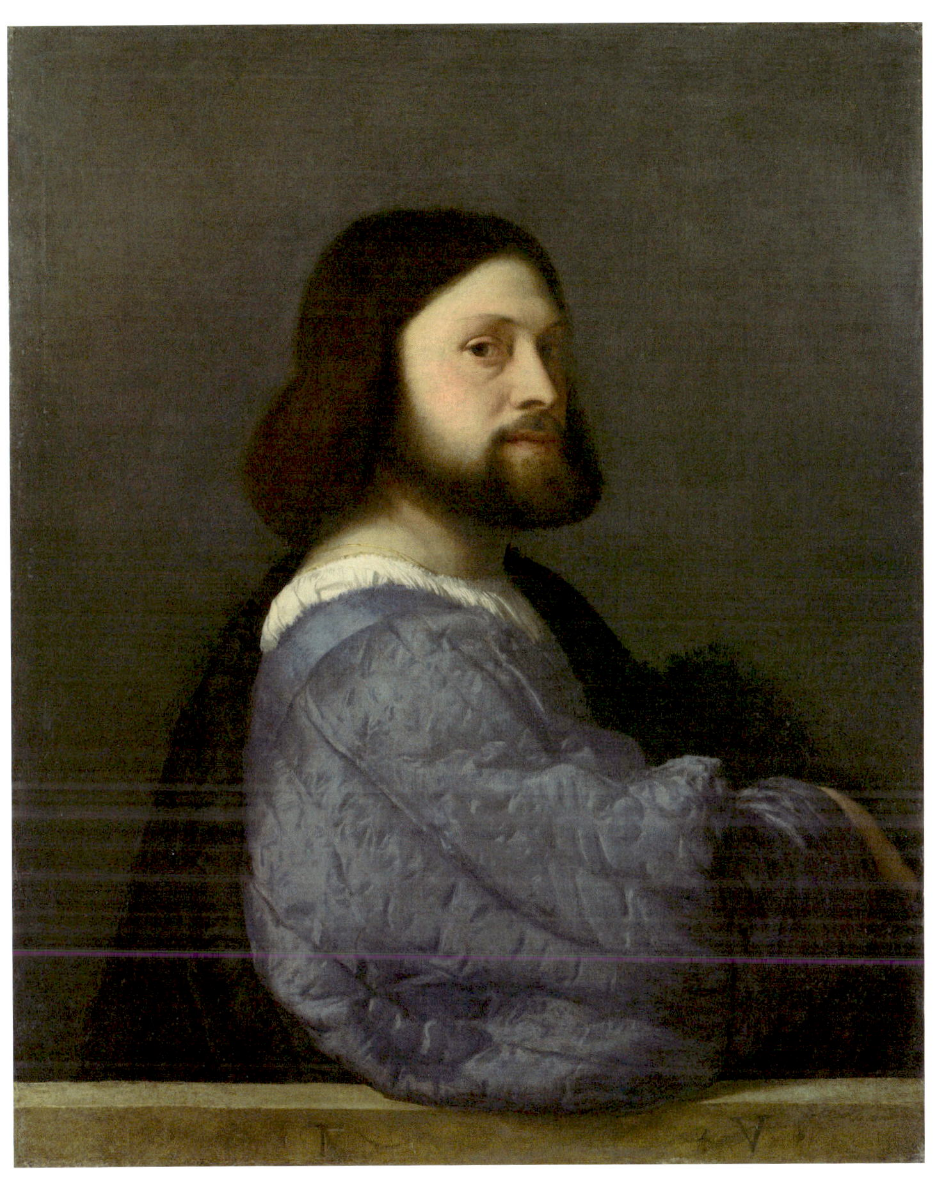

35. Titian, *Portrait of Gerolamo (?)
Barbarigo*, about 1510.

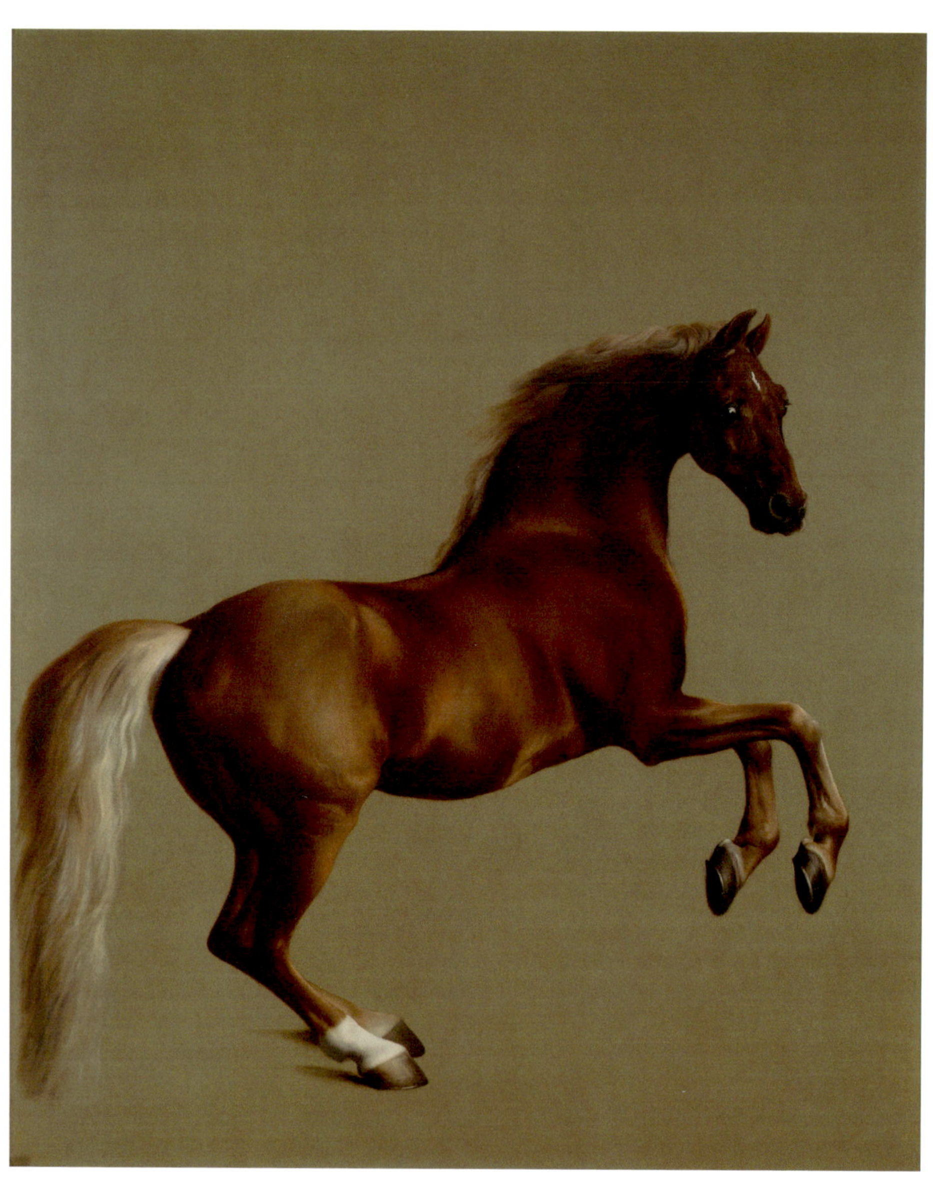

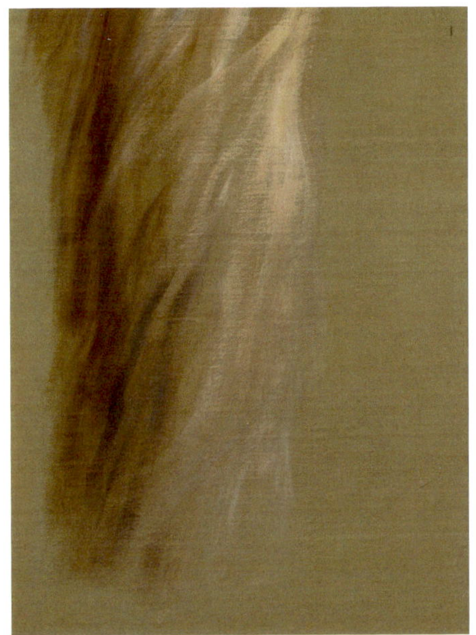 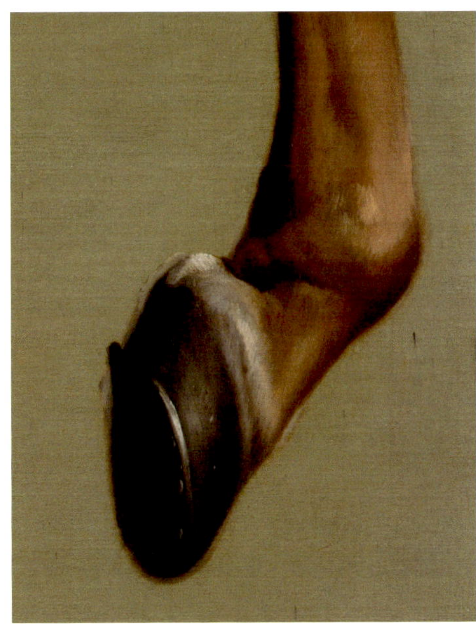

36. George Stubbs, *Whistlejacket*, about 1762. It seems likely that the horse's tail was originally partly covered by the painting's frame.

37 and 38. Details from *Whistlejacket*.

represents, or rather evokes, real space [36]. The colour is close to that of a sandy soil and, as we see from the short shadows behind his rear hoofs, the stallion is standing on it. But the colour also has an airy character that vibrates round the hoofs and infiltrates the tail as it moves [37, 38]. Many explanations could be advanced for why the painter proposed, and his patron accepted, this unusual setting. An architectural explanation would be that such a background suited the plain walls of the room at Wentworth Woodhouse in which it was to be the only painting; a sculptural explanation would emphasise the relationship to the monumental antique marble sculptures and fine bronze statuettes of horses in Lord Rockingham's possession; a pictorial one would note that, in a painting designed to hang at such a great height, a landscape setting might have seemed wrong. The origin of the idea is easier to guess: some of Stubbs's portraits of horses were intended to have landscape settings by other artists and would have left his studio in this state.

If we were to measure Whistlejacket's outline on the canvas, the horse would be smaller than we know it to have been, but this is of course because it is depicted as if more than a foot from the front plane of the painting. So it may be said to be a life-size image. As such, it had a great, even an alarming, impact. Whistlejacket himself was said to have been agitated by the sight of it when it was being painted, and sophisticated visitors to

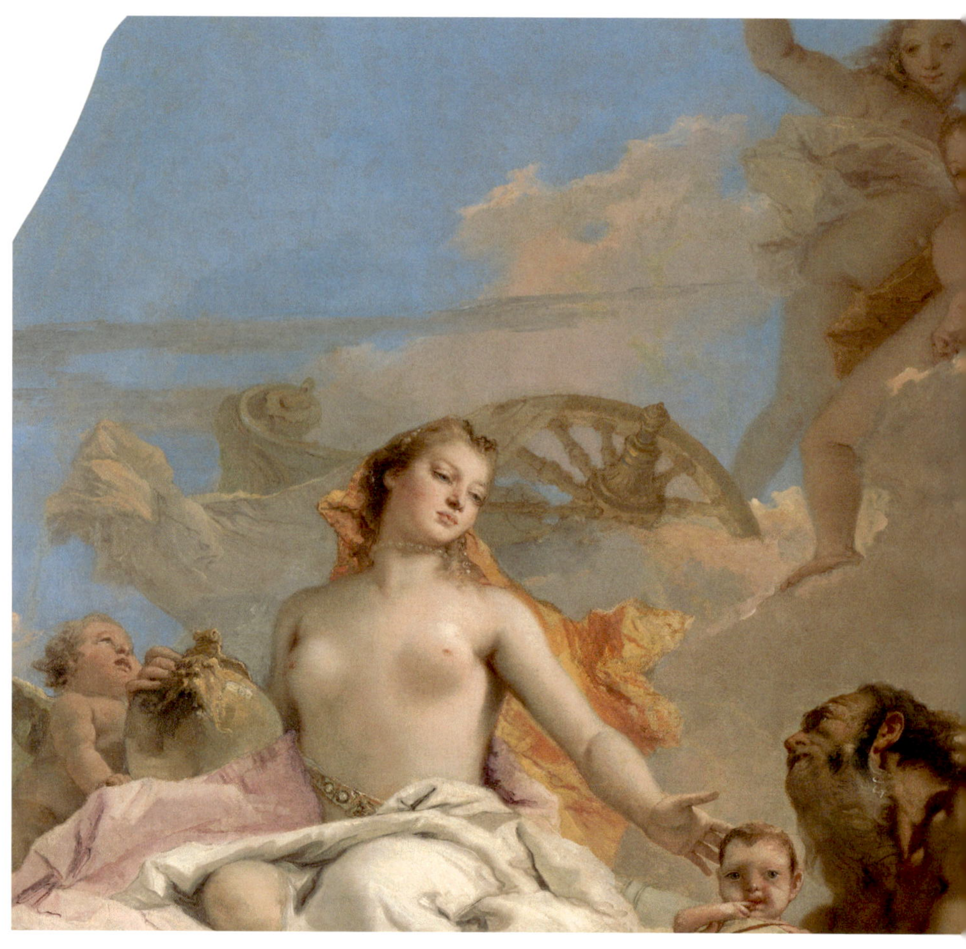

Wentworth Woodhouse professed to believe, albeit momentarily, that it was alive.

Ceiling paintings often incorporated fictive architecture elements that continued those of the room for which they were painted, but such exercises in linear perspective only make sense if the viewer is standing in a particular place in the room below, and from any other position the architecture can seem awkward or even absurd. Giambattista Tiepolo, one of the greatest of all painters of heavenly scenery both sacred and profane, preferred to shrink or banish such fictive architectural components. In his *Allegory with Venus and Time* [40], space is suggested by reducing the size of the figures and the intensity of the colours. Richer and darker pigments are employed for the elements of the painting that would be lower and closer to the viewer – charcoal

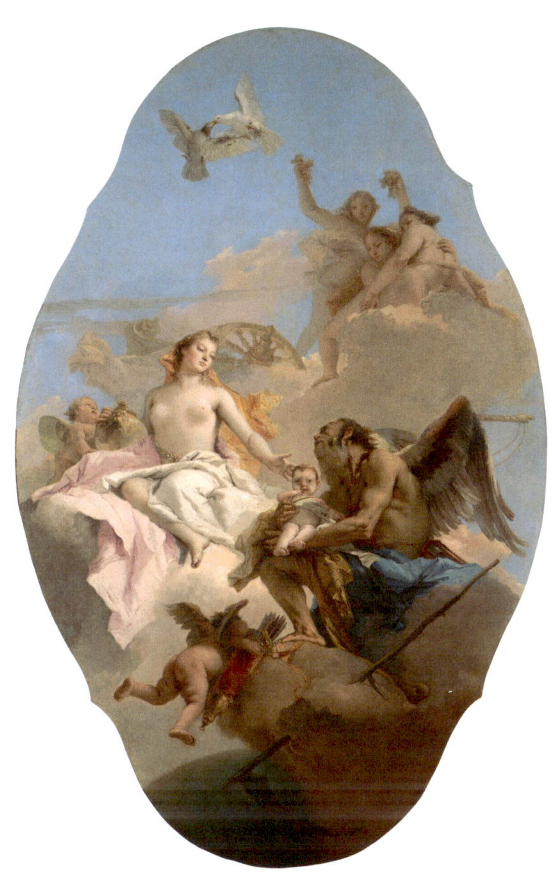

39 (detail) and 40. Giovanni Battista Tiepolo, *Allegory with Venus and Time,* about 1754–8.

grey in the hair and wings of Father Time, deep blue for the shadows of his cloak, russet red in Cupid's quiver, an intense green for the sphere of the Earth below; far above, the three intertwined Graces blend, in both form and colour, with the soft, plump clouds by which they are supported. The composition is constructed of curves that echo the cusped oval shape of the canvas: the doves billing in mid-flight, the wheel of Venus' chariot, the vase the goddess bears, the sweeping wings of Time, and the great curved blade of his scythe. But there is, in addition, a scaffolding of diagonals in a zigzag arrangement, beginning with the pole of the scythe, continuing in the outstretched arm of Venus consigning the child to Time (or conferring upon the child her blessing), and continued in the slightly tilted bar of cloud beside the Graces.

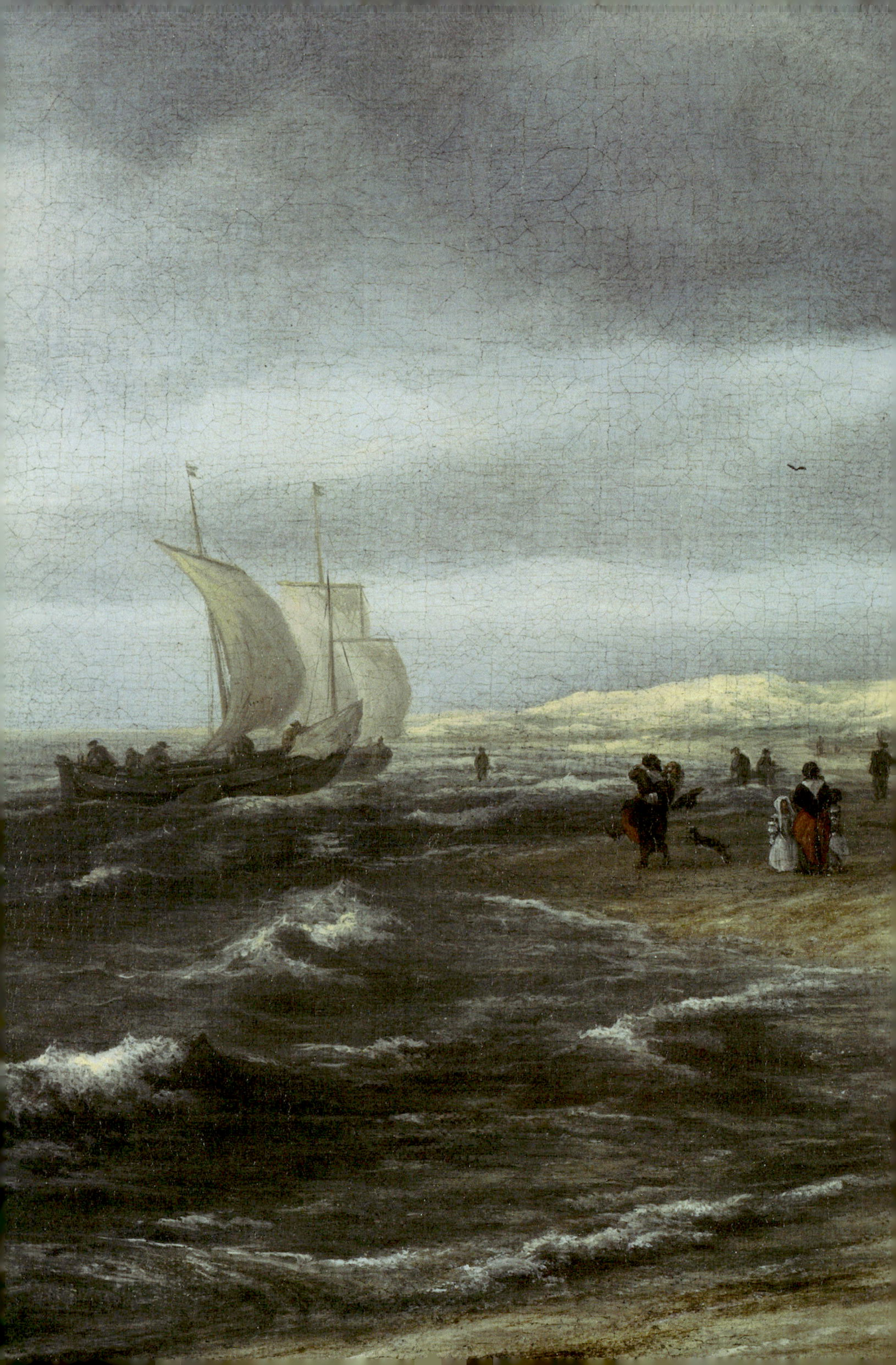

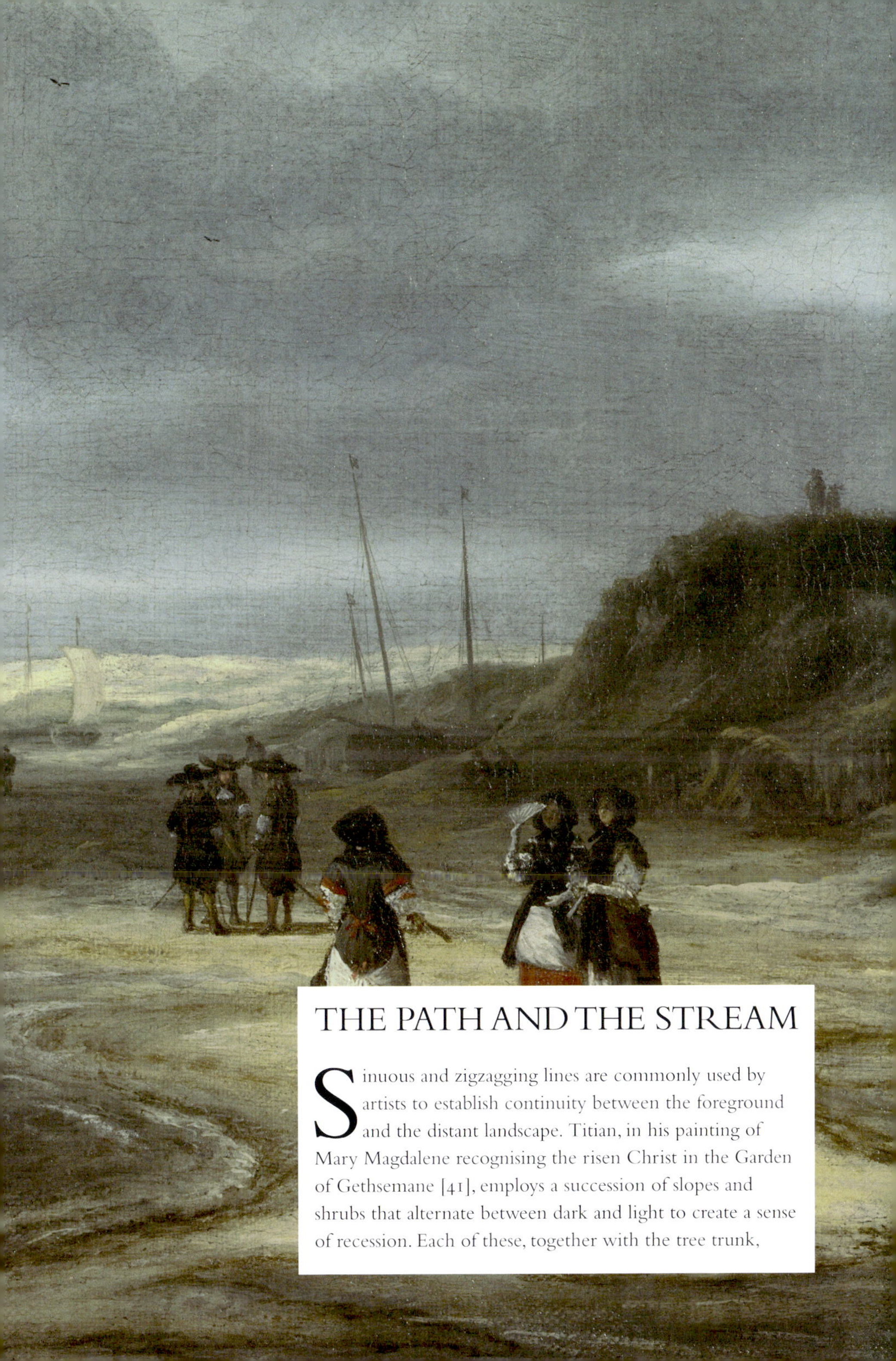

THE PATH AND THE STREAM

Sinuous and zigzagging lines are commonly used by
artists to establish continuity between the foreground
and the distant landscape. Titian, in his painting of
Mary Magdalene recognising the risen Christ in the Garden
of Gethsemane [41], employs a succession of slopes and
shrubs that alternate between dark and light to create a sense
of recession. Each of these, together with the tree trunk,

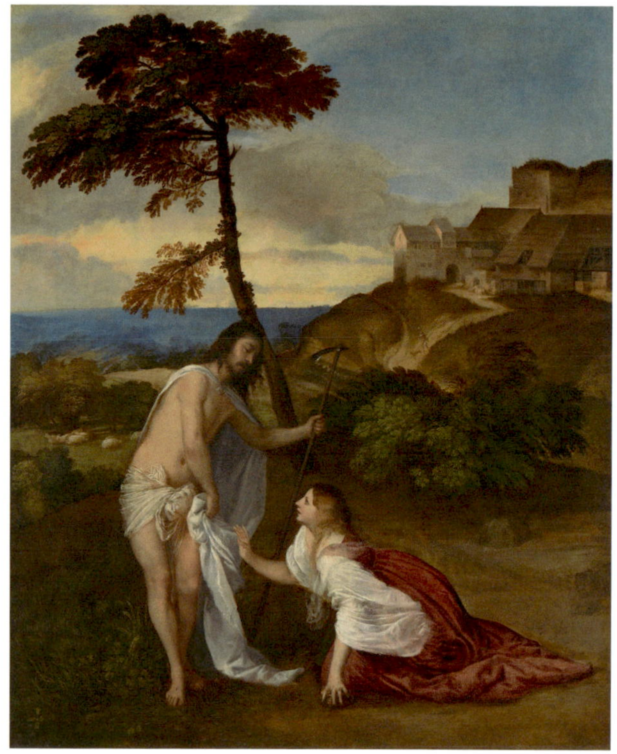

is closely related to the shapes and movements of the figures in
the foreground. On the left side of the painting indistinct green
forms begin to lose themselves in the blue haze; on the right,
the ground rises and paths wind uphill to the clustered farm
buildings partly lit by the early morning sun [42]. The buildings
appear faint – in accordance with aerial perspective – but are
painted with exquisite detail, for instance in the spacing of the
rough planks screening the openings. It is the curving paths that
connect the buildings with the foreground, not merely by their
form but by their colour, which is surprisingly close to that of
the near-naked body of the risen Christ.

During the seventeenth century, landscape painting came
to be fully established as an independent genre, and humble
scenery of the kind that we see in Titian's painting had become
a subject in its own right, especially in Holland (although the
local landscape included few hills). In Jacob van Ruisdael's view
of the seashore near Egmond-aan-Zee [43], we may not be
immediately aware of some of the devices he uses to enhance
the sense of recession in the painting, including the swept line

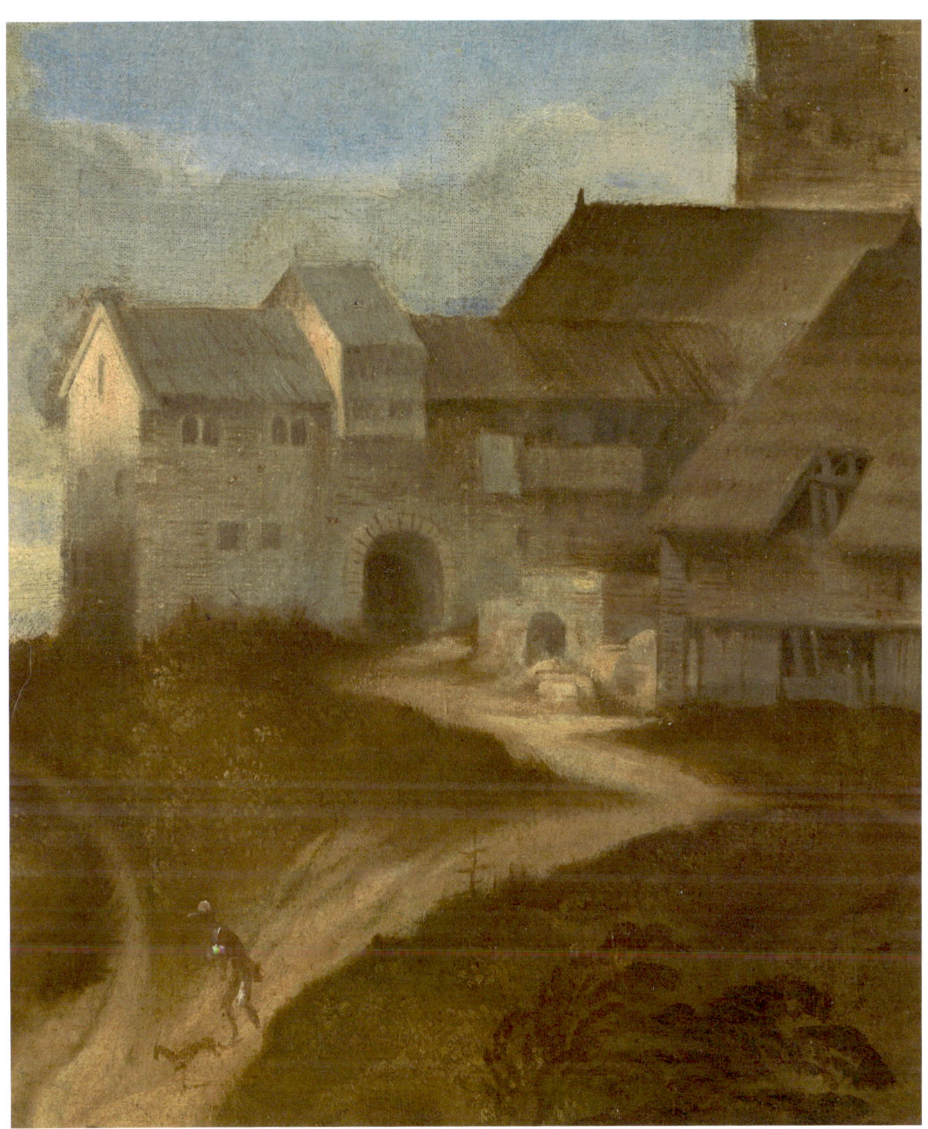

42. Detail from *Noli me tangere*. The farm buildings represented here are probably based on a drawing which Titian used on two other occasions.

of the water's edge, the repetition of lines in the footpaths or tracks in the sand, and the larger curling shapes of the clouds, which cast a shadow over the dunes in the middle distance. We are perhaps more alert to the way that the diminishing size of the figures helps to conduct us into the distance. First, there is a group of three women fashionably attired in black, white and red and carrying fans (which they surely do not need); next, three men, perhaps their husbands; and then, further in the

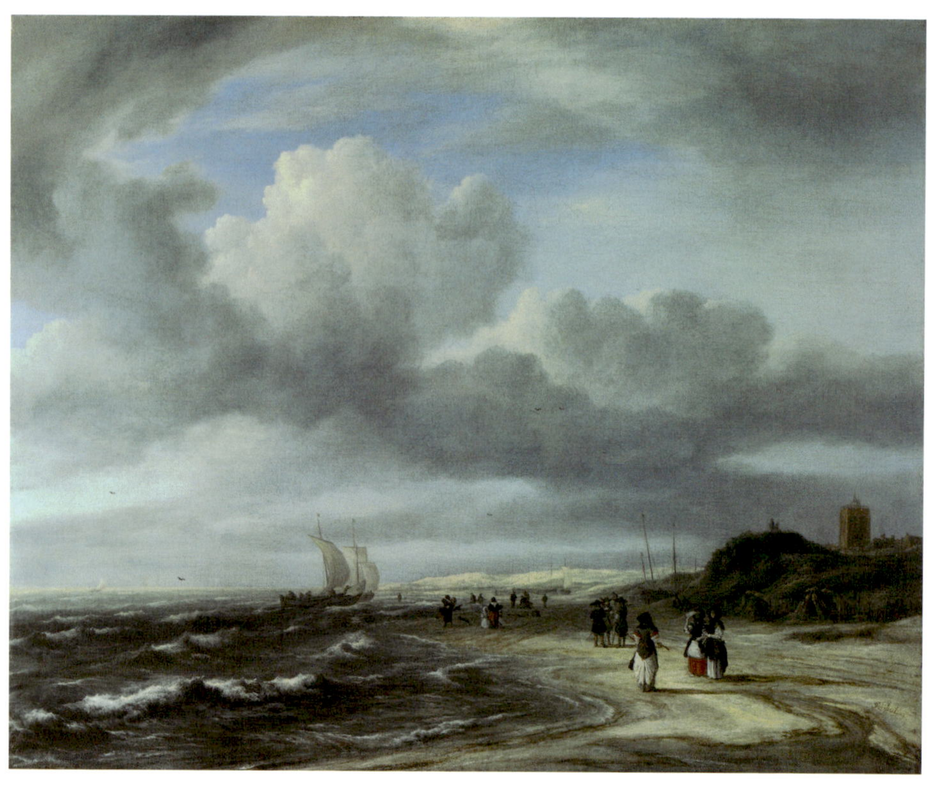

43. Jacob van Ruisdael, *The Shore at Egmond-aan-Zee,* about 1675.

distance, a miscellany of figures, including a child and a dog. These seem to be by the hand of another artist (perhaps Gerard van Betten) but, even had they been painted by Ruisdael, they would surely have been added last to what was chiefly a landscape.

A stream can sometimes become a path when the water runs dry in summer, and that is what we see winding through the rocky foreground in Poussin's painting with the misleading title of *Landscape with Travellers Resting* [44]. The men are seated on banks that would be very surprising beside a road or track. A side path for use in winter when torrential water fills the river bed can be seen to the left, following a tighter, serpentine line. The three figures help to define the space by their diminishing size but they also suggest the hardship and even the dangers of travelling. The traveller in the foreground is not really resting. He grasps his staff purposefully and his other hand is pressed to the ground as he turns to look at the man behind him, who is seated and bending forward, perhaps to adjust a sandal. They seem to have been walking towards the

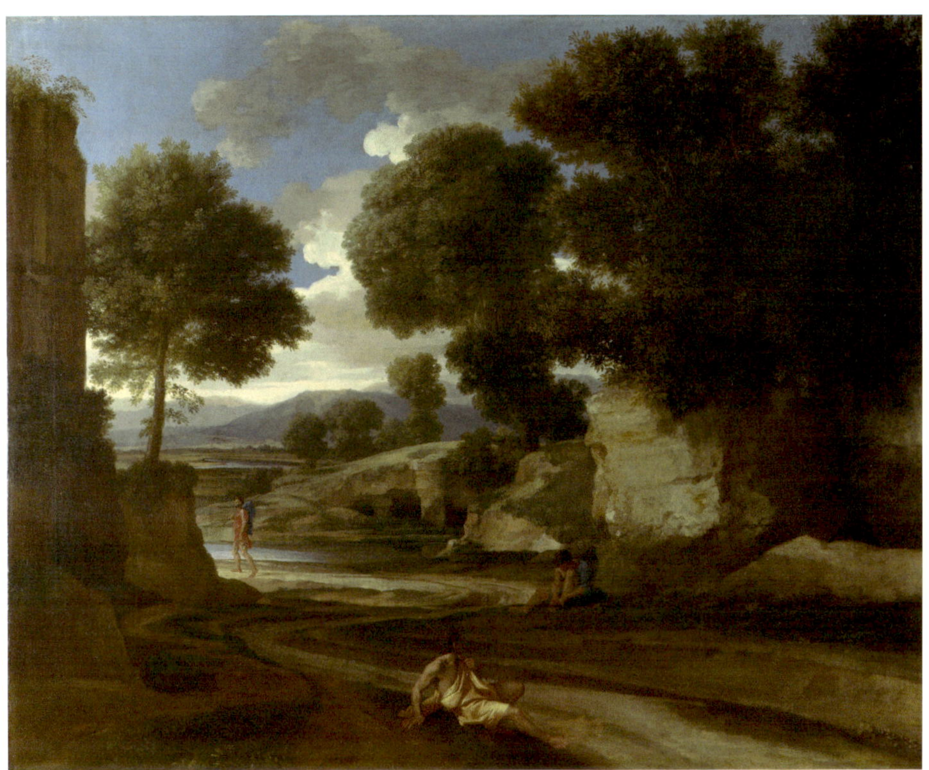

viewer. The third man, who walks away in the middle distance, does so with awareness of them, and perhaps also with concern. As a great narrative painter Poussin may have found it hard to resist a suggestion of some relationship or interaction. As in other paintings by him, the passage into the landscape seems like a puzzle that needs to be solved by the human beings. Here water blocks the way – probably a broad river with rocky banks. Its winding course, or that of a tributary, is probably represented by the light reflecting on the water in the plain beyond. If we can reach the plain by following the river, the way will be level and hospitality will await us in the town just barely visible in the distance.

Far less usual as a spatial device is the straight road set at a right-angle to the front plane of the picture. In Meindert Hobbema's *Avenue at Middelharnis* the road is straight but rough with irregular and sinuous wheel tracks [45]. There are ditches to either side of the road, the waters of which have fed the rows of fast-growing pollarded poplars. The artist, who originally began the colonnade of trees with two that were even nearer to

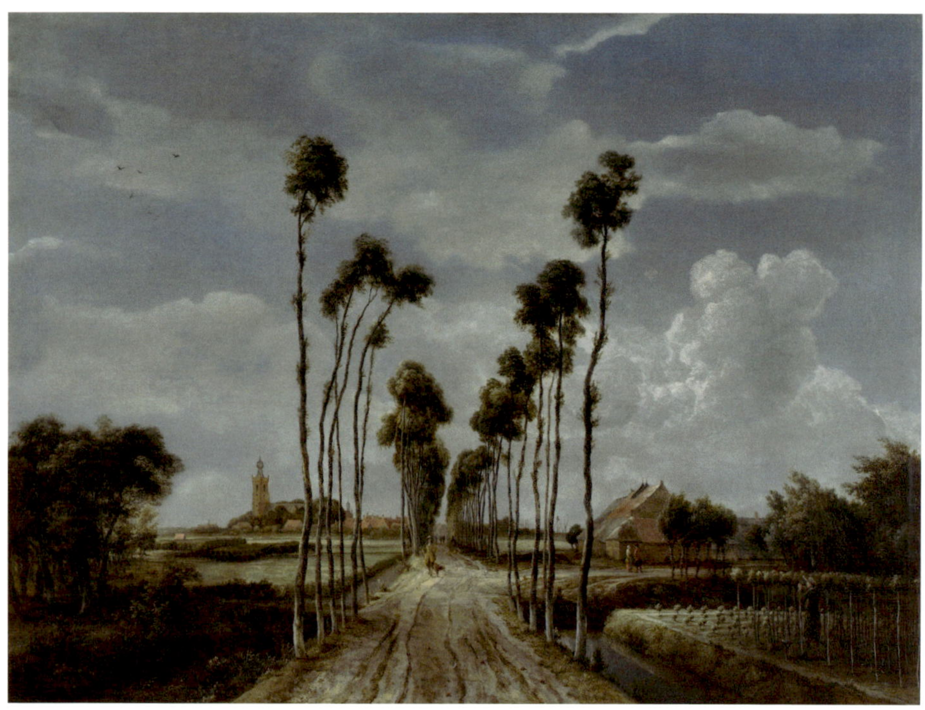

45. Meindert Hobbema, *The Avenue at Middelharnis*, 1689.

46. Detail from *The Avenue at Middelharnis*. The dog in its original position was painted out but has begun to reappear (on account of the increasing transparency of the paint) in the road between us and the strolling man.

us, was careful to provide incident outside this vertical portion of his canvas – notably the nurseryman tending his potted saplings. Our eyes are also drawn to the horizon, to the church on the left and, less obvious on the right, the masts of distant ships. But our attention always returns to the avenue, where a man is advancing towards us with gun and dog. We will meet him halfway. It is delightful to note from careful examination of the road that the dog was originally placed considerably in front of its owner as if it were hastening to greet us [46]. But even without this detail 'we are drawn', in Erika Langmuir's words, 'companionably into his picture'. This only works, of course, if the viewer's eyes are level with, or slightly below, the vanishing point. Artists such as Hobbema would have expected their paintings to be hung at a greater height than is usual today, and the effects of recession that they hoped to achieve are often frustrated.

The Impressionists gave new life to landscape painting in the 1860s and 1870s by bringing the finished picture closer to the oil sketch. And because their paintings were often made, or at least begun, outdoors they avoided complex and intricate subjects. Yet we meet the same conventions for spatial recession. A good example is Claude Monet's view of the 'Petit Bras' of

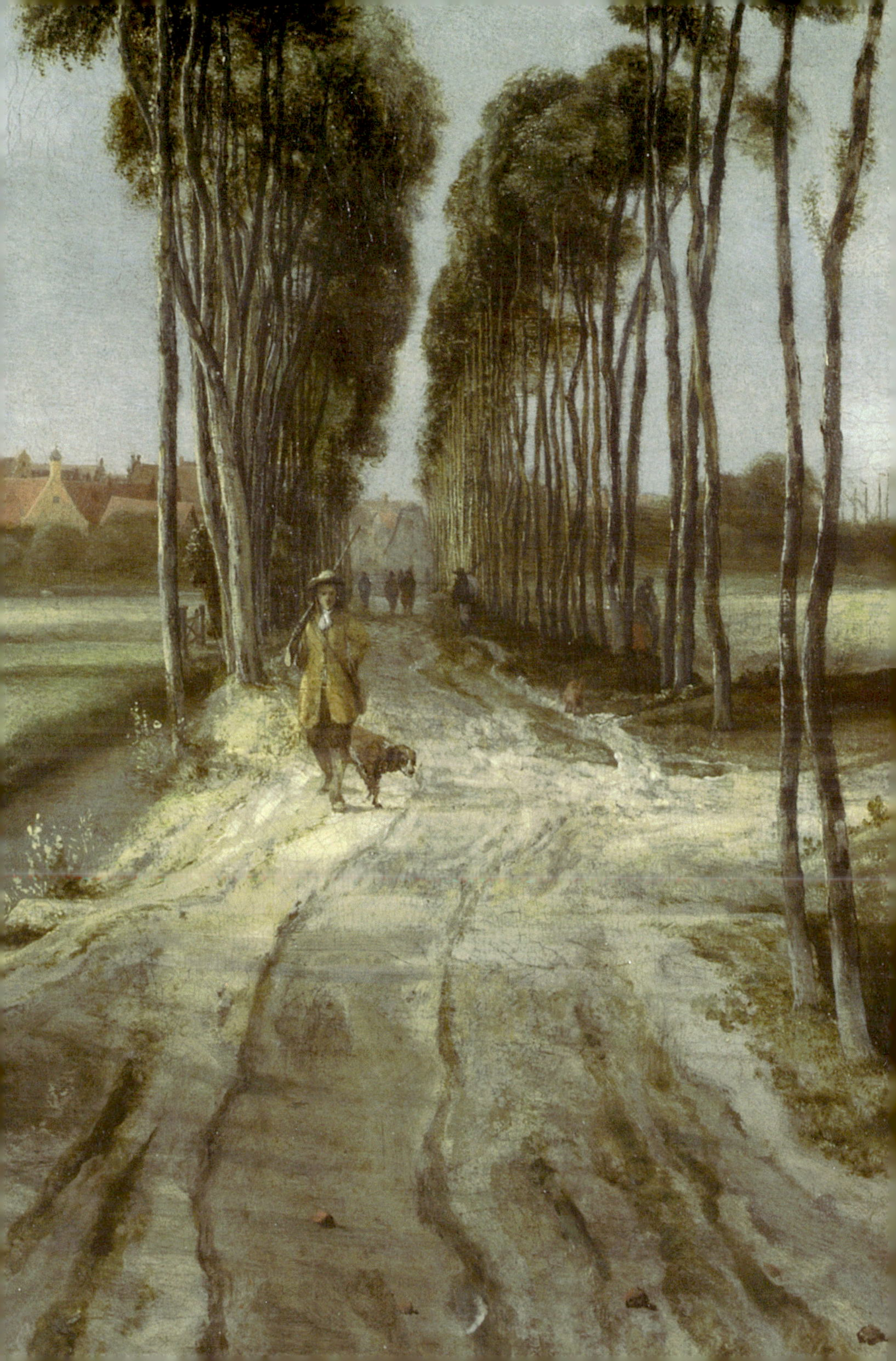

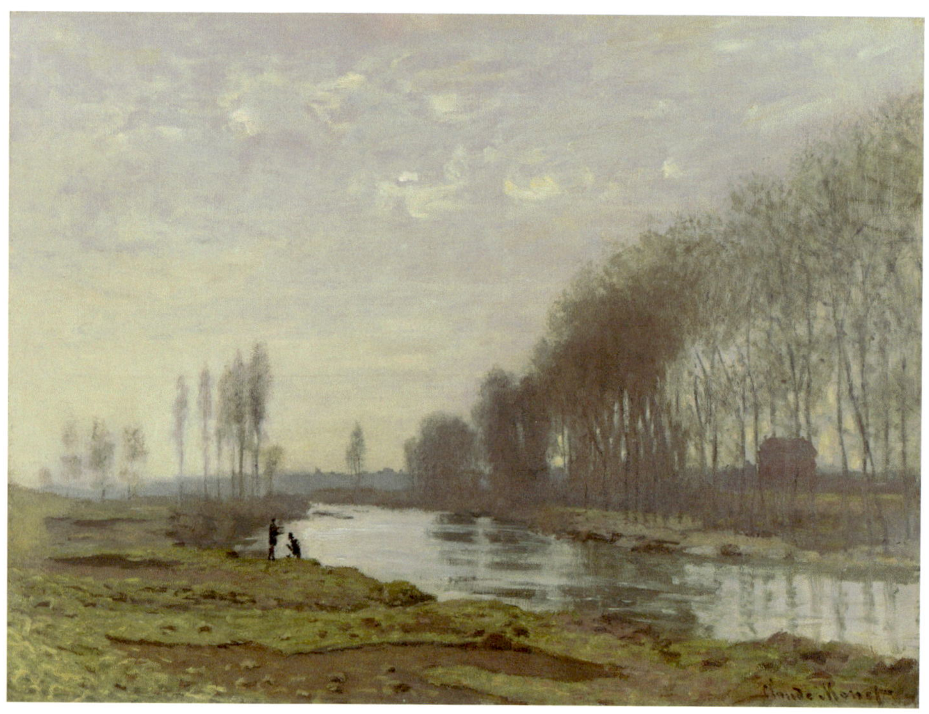

the Seine near Argenteuil [47] with its row of poplars, its
winding river and its figures, added last, to define the distance.
In this case the figures are certainly by the same artist as the
landscape. Monet was a master of the lively and witty silhouette
(they look to me like fishermen untangling a line) but also
understood how distant figures can seem fragmented by bright
light. Here they are very small but impossible to miss because
they are by far the darkest patches of paint in the picture,
providing an extremely effective foil to the pale greys and silvery
blue and violet brown around them, and contrasting in their
jagged precision with the smudged verticals of the trees rising
like smoke behind them [48].

At a slightly earlier date Camille Pissarro painted pleasing
views of the tree-lined streets and railway lines of the south
London suburbs, adding figures for scale and human interest,
but in 1877, painting a hillside near his home at Pontoise
[49], he created a canvas which is extraordinary for its visual
confusion. It is as if the suspension of prior knowledge that
was essential to much aerial perspective – painting the distant
green trees as purplish-grey smoke, for example – has been
extended to all the visual data before him. Certainly the usual

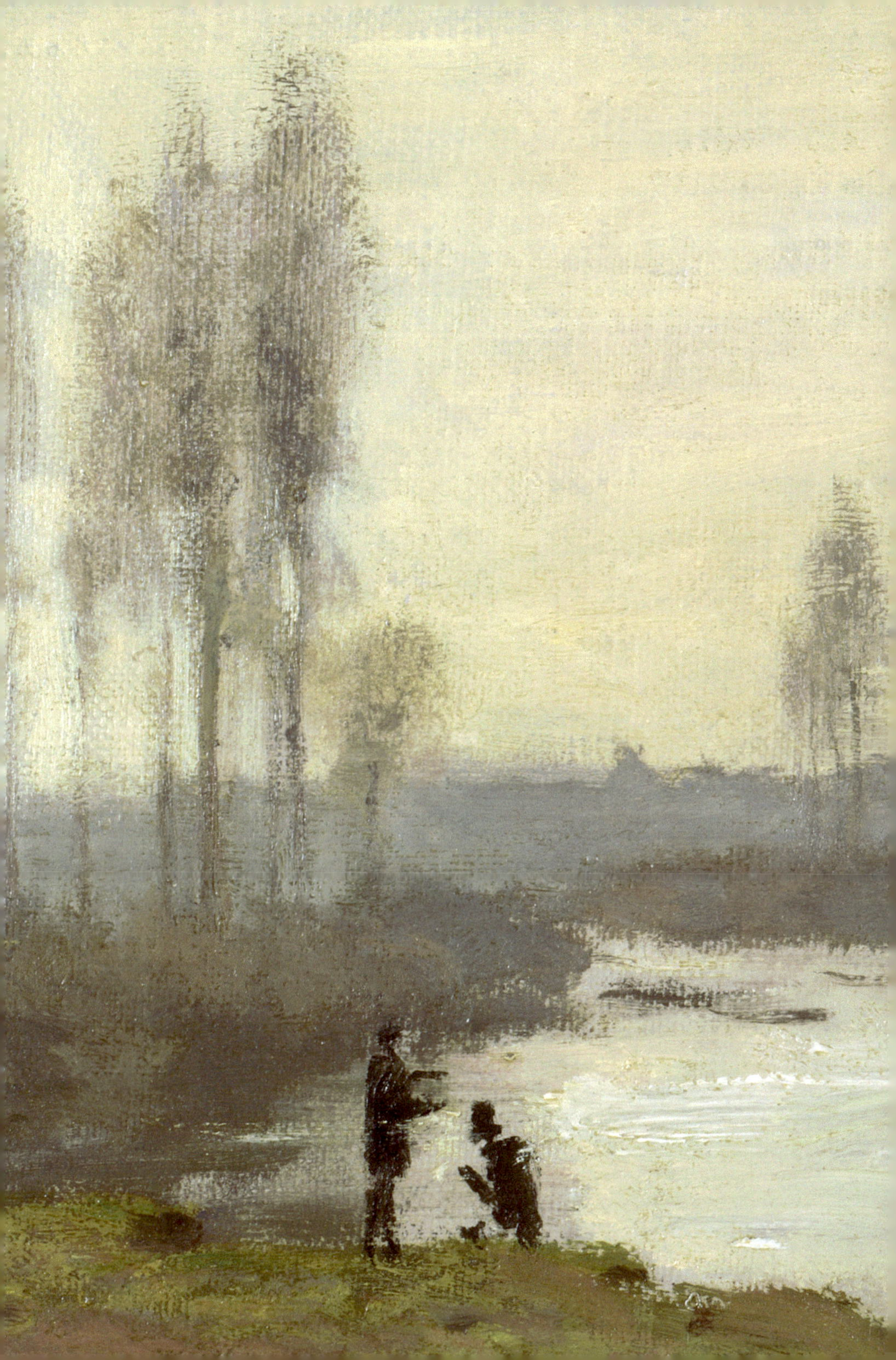

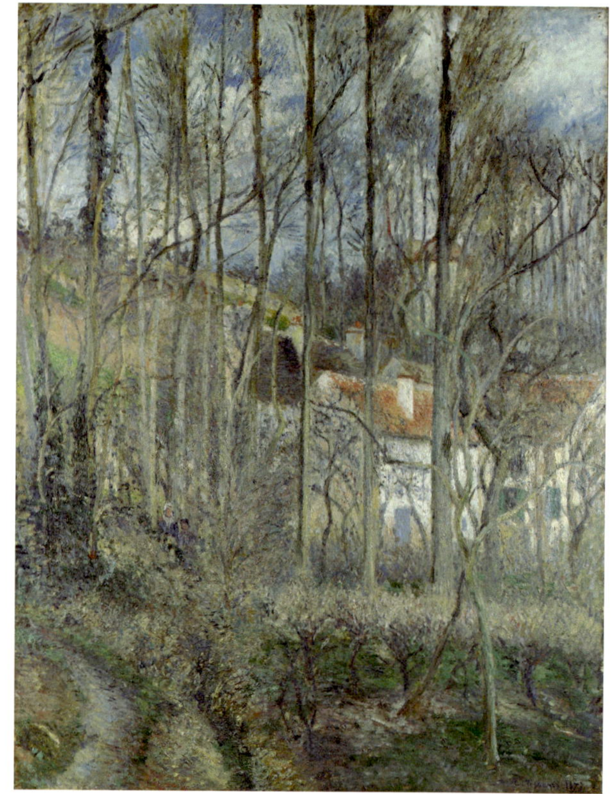

devices are discarded. There is a path but it makes only a feeble
attempt to penetrate into pictorial space and then curls off,
as if in despair. There are also some figures but they are on no
discernible track and it is hard to tell exactly where they are
standing. A screen of trees crosses the painting in the middle
distance but one tree in the foreground, a sapling with a prop
supporting it, has its upper branches interwoven with those of
the thickest tree in the screen and with those of another very
crooked tree behind it. Higher up, the branches of all three trees
are lost – or almost lost – among the trunks of fifteen or more
in the distance. Because of the trees, we cannot be sure of the
shapes of the whitewashed farm buildings on the right, nor can
we tell how they relate to each other. When we step back we
find a compositional pattern created by branches curving to the
right, as if to counter the sweep of the path, lower left, but it is
a pattern without spatial force. It seems to be part of the almost
woven texture of the surface created by the dense impasto of
the paint [50, 51].

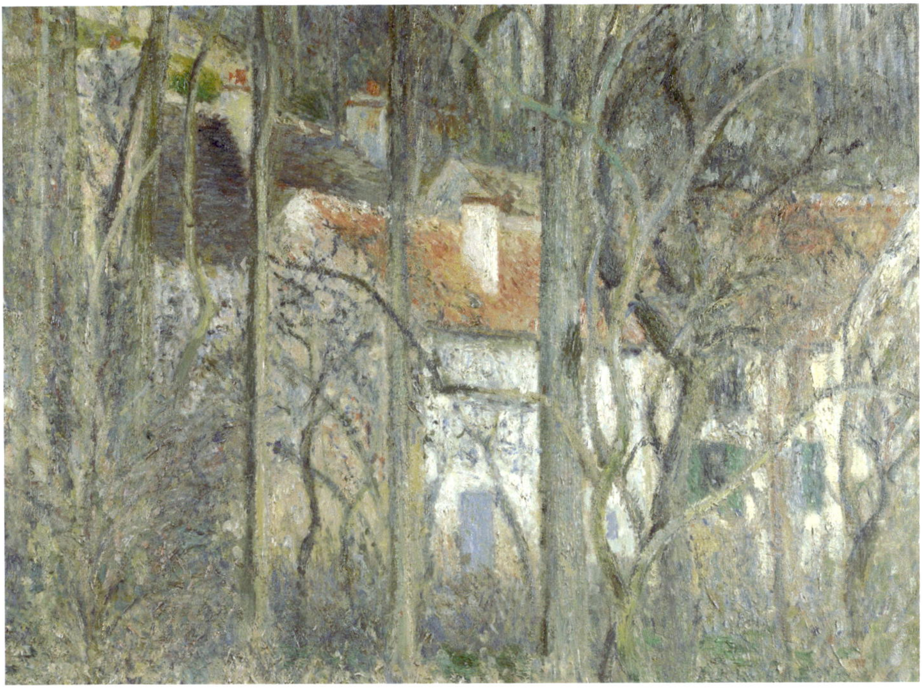

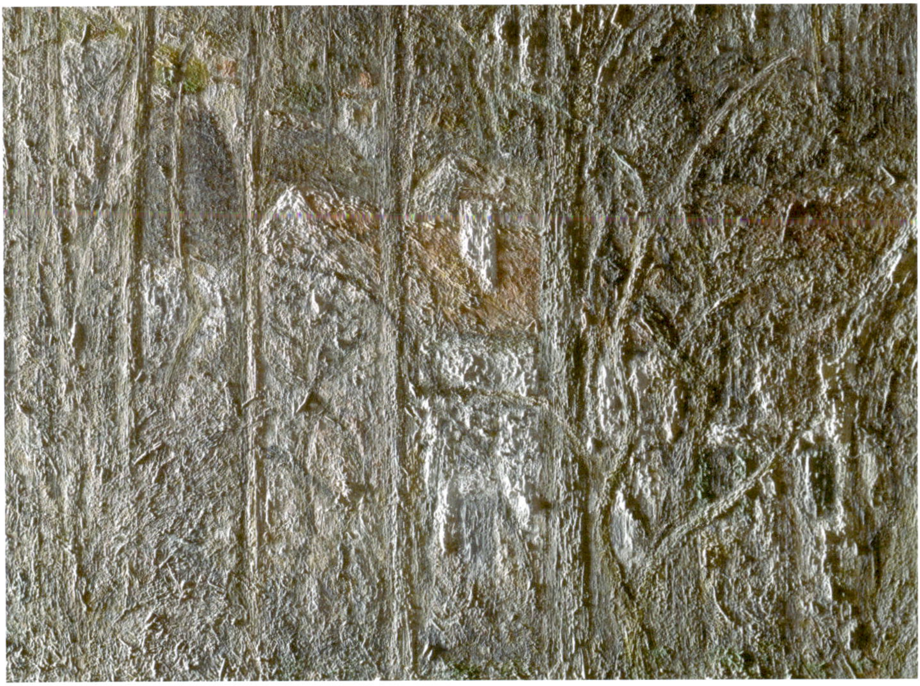

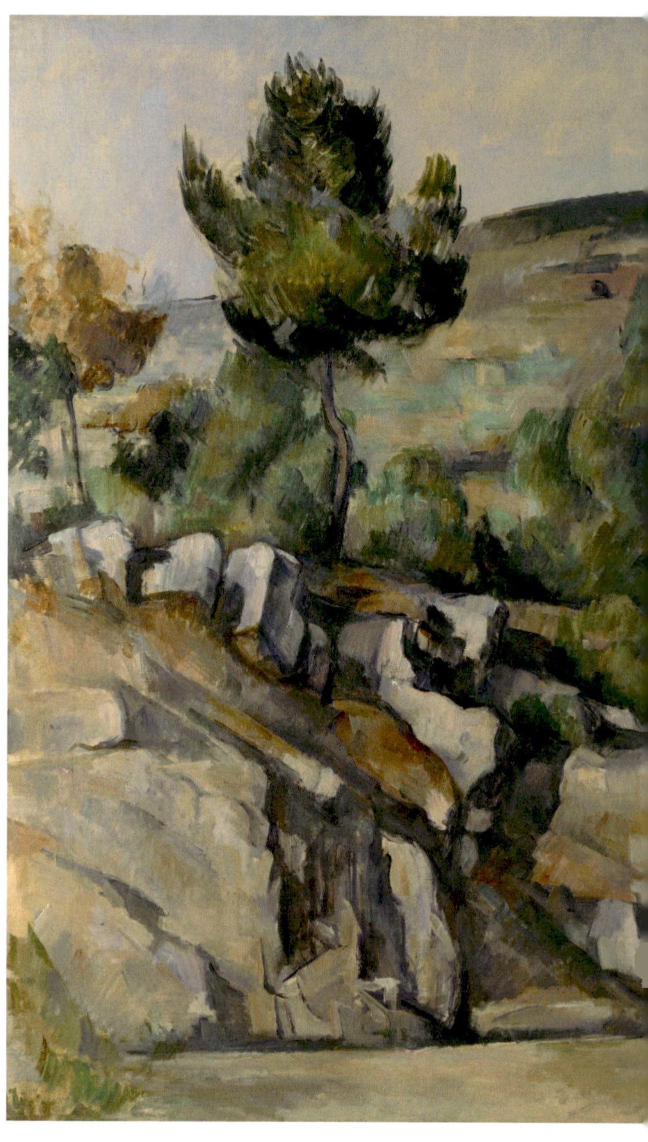

It seems likely that this daring way of painting was at least partly influenced by Cézanne, who was staying with Pissarro at this date. Cézanne's own later achievement as a landscape painter is well illustrated by his *Hillside in Provence* [52]. The road in the foreground could easily be mistaken for a stream. It does not take us anywhere. Nor does it provide a stable preliminary platform because it is not quite parallel with the picture plane. Behind, or rather above, there is a wall of rock that may be the

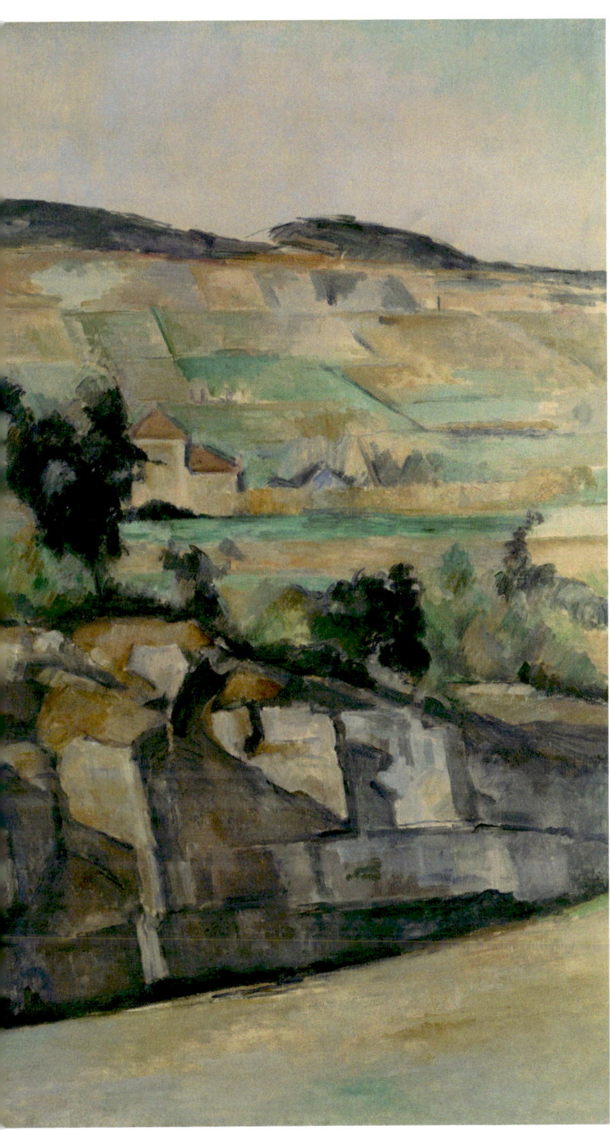

52. Paul Cézanne, *Hillside in Provence*, about 1890–2.

debris of a quarry or an outcrop naturally breaking into blocks, but blocks with no horizontal or vertical faces, or indeed any complete outlines. Beyond, there is a hillside covered by fields in a rectangular pattern, but the outlines of the fields are discontinuous; even when parallel, they do not converge. And then there is the curving line of the hill which answers the curve of the road in the foreground.

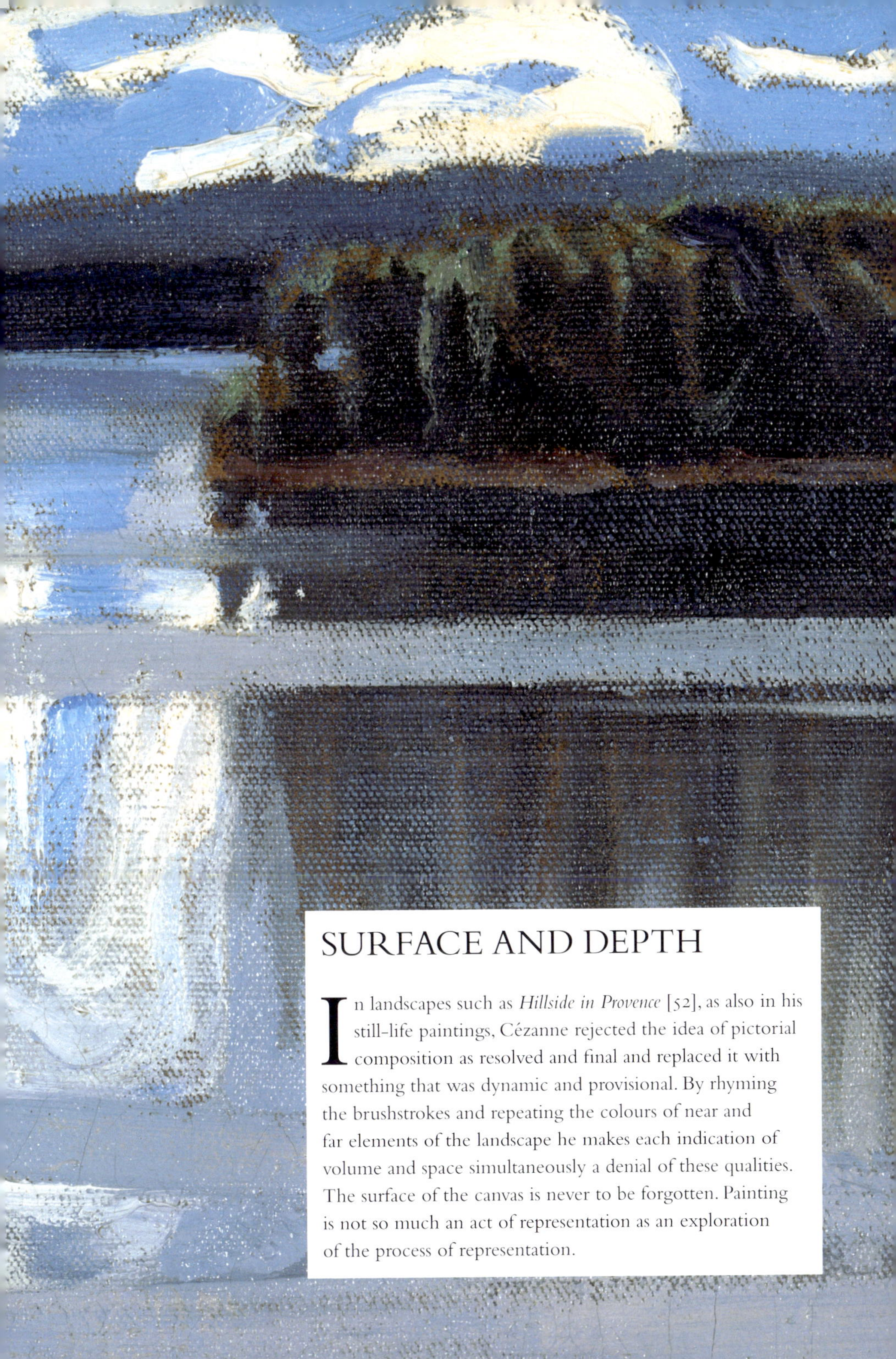

SURFACE AND DEPTH

In landscapes such as *Hillside in Provence* [52], as also in his still-life paintings, Cézanne rejected the idea of pictorial composition as resolved and final and replaced it with something that was dynamic and provisional. By rhyming the brushstrokes and repeating the colours of near and far elements of the landscape he makes each indication of volume and space simultaneously a denial of these qualities. The surface of the canvas is never to be forgotten. Painting is not so much an act of representation as an exploration of the process of representation.

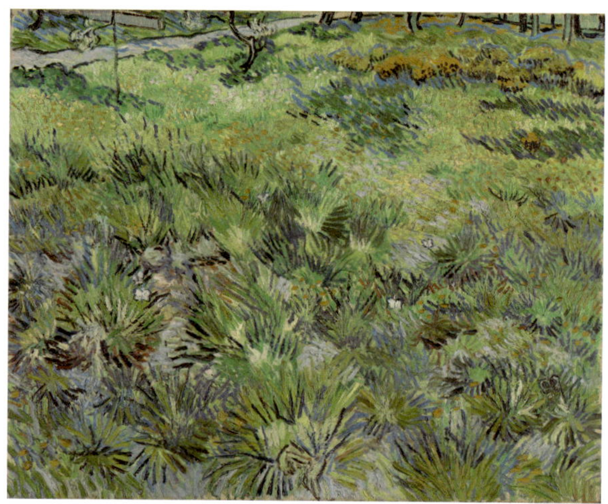

There are other ways in which the picture surface can be emphasised at the expense of fictive space. One device is the adoption of a high viewpoint so that there is no horizon line in the painting. In Van Gogh's *Long Grass with Butterflies*, for example, recession is indicated by the diminishing size of the brushstrokes with which each explosion of blades is rendered, and then, at the very top of the picture, by including the bases of a few tree trunks beside a path [53]. Every stroke is made with a loaded brush (between the strokes the bare canvas is occasionally visible). This way of handling paint was perhaps derived from drawing with a reed pen; its impact depends on speed of execution and on the energy of each stroke. The effect is powerful, although not in every respect a success, certainly not in the heavy white squiggles that represent butterflies fluttering over the grass [54, 55].

Some of Monet's late paintings of lily ponds are still more remarkable in that the surface of the pond corresponds to the surface of the canvas, and is full of reflected light and space. These works are very uneven in quality, some of the least successful being among those which are most admired today because of their fortuitous resemblance to the paintings made in New York by the Abstract Expressionists half a century later, but the one illustrated here has a mesmerising fascination [56]. The pink and yellow of the sunset (a combination of colours worthy of Giovanni Battista Tiepolo) is rubbed over a layer of pale lilac grey, imitating the way reflected light can seem to float on water [57]. Only the foreground reeds strike a false note, as if the artist retreated from the radical character of his

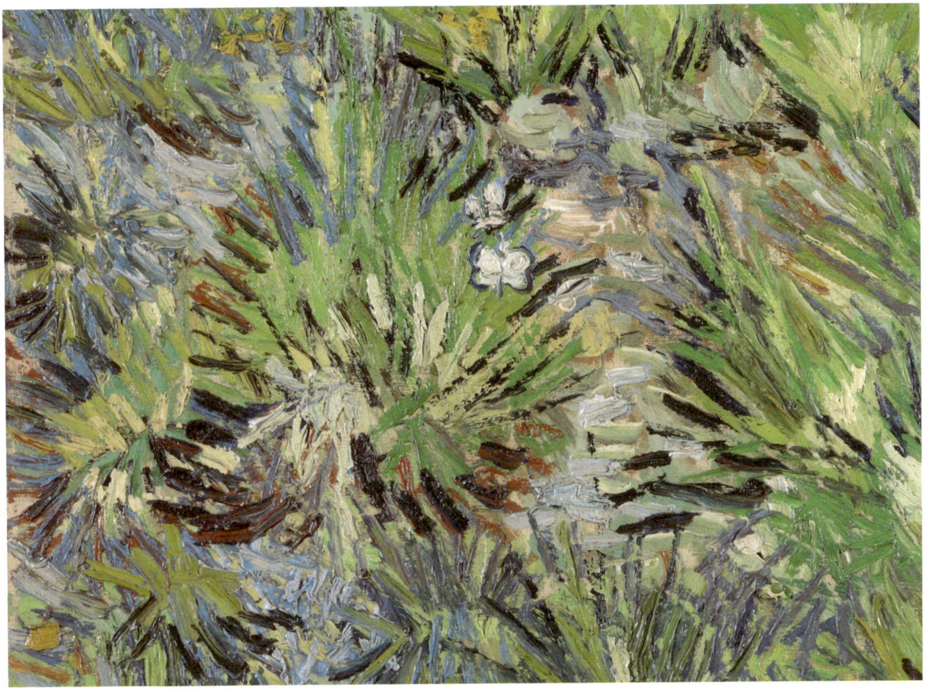

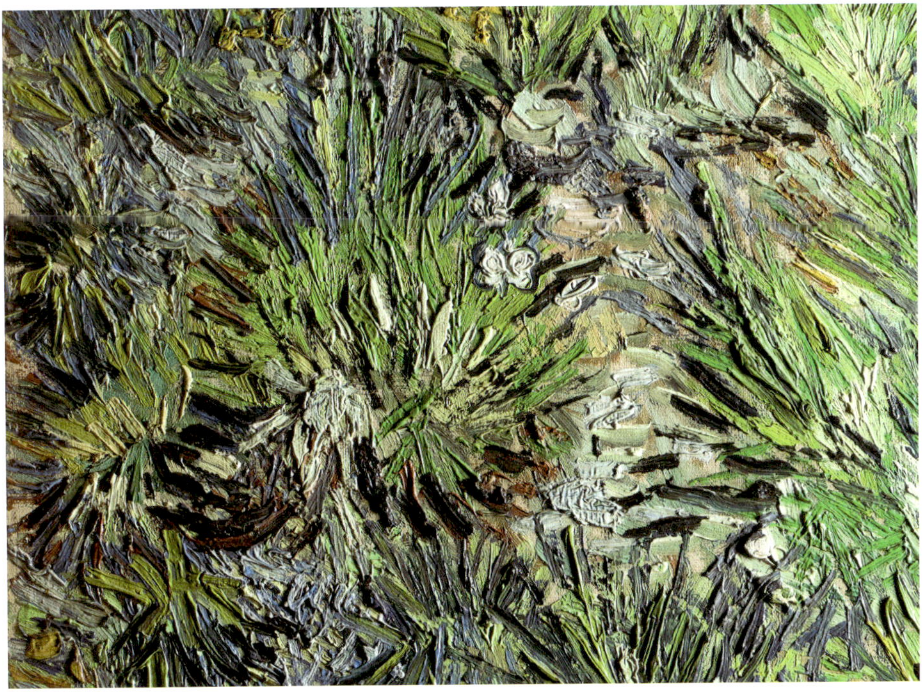

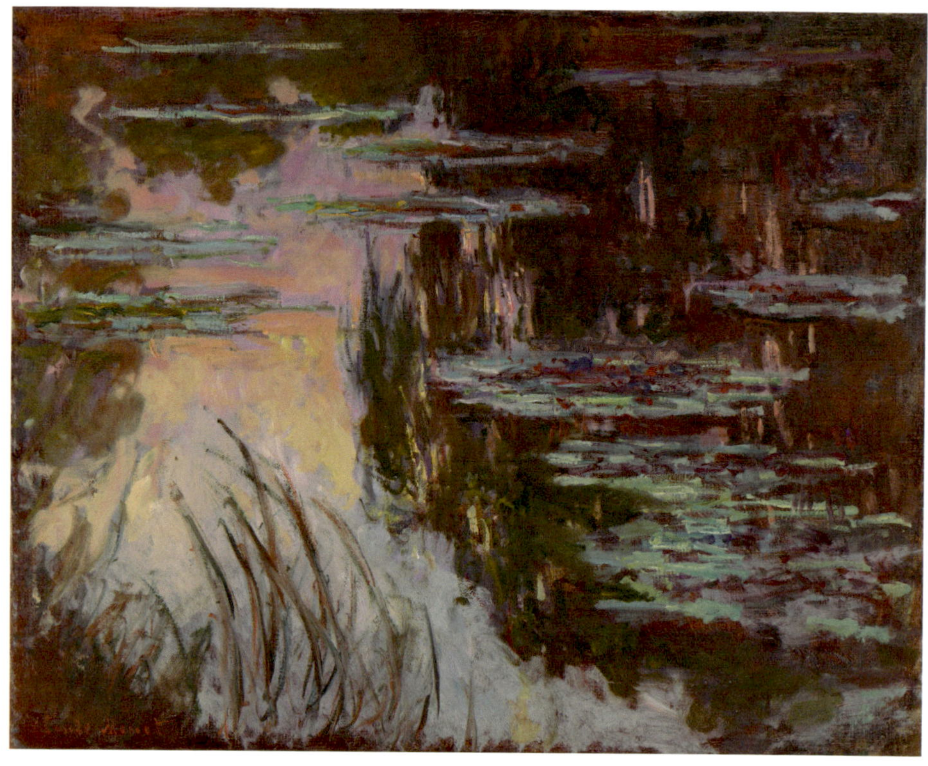

56 and 57 (detail). Claude Monet, *Water-Lilies, Setting Sun*, about 1907.

invention and decided to give us some small patch of land on which to stand.

Another painting of that period which consists in large part of reflections and has a very high horizon line is the view of Lake Keitele by the Finnish artist Akseli Gallen-Kallela [58]. It makes much of the uncanny in nature – the way that reflections and shadows can seem like tall, spectral doubles and the way a breeze can disturb the surface of the water to suggest the passage over it of some being or spirit. In this case the bands on the surface are contrasted in texture with the rest of the water. They are sufficiently diagonal for us to think of them as zigzagging, and diminish in width just enough to create a compelling sense of recession that counters the pattern of vertical reflections.

In the strip of sky, clouds of uniform white without volume dance against an unmodified blue without depth, creating a pattern that seems to jump forward and reassert the flatness of the painting. Vitality is added by the movement of the brush and by the presence here of another colour – that of the brown underlayer – which is not quite covered by the thick blue and

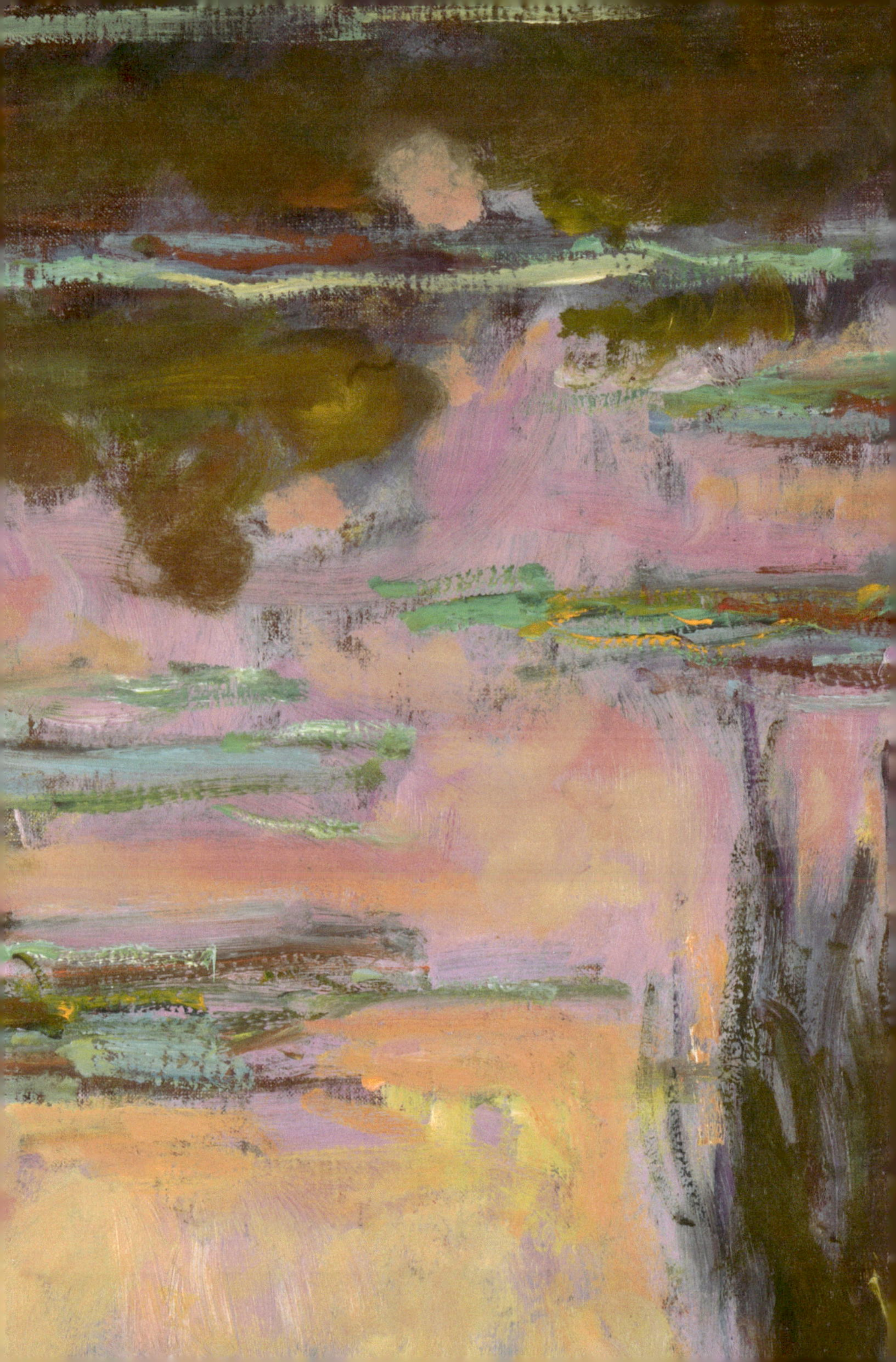

white paint and forms a ragged fringe around the positive and negative shapes of clouds and sky.

Psychologically this painting incorporates a spatial effect of a kind that we have not previously encountered in this book: the sensation of something seen when we look back or turn round. This may be because water fills the foreground, as it would if we were looking from a boat on the water, and it is when we are on a boat that we are more likely to be aware of what lies behind us than when travelling by any other means.

Another influence in the way artists thought about space came from the style of mural decoration that was preferred for architecture, especially, at first, for churches in the neo-Romanesque or neo-Gothic style, where it was felt that an insistent recession, and indeed any detailed realism, might disturb the aesthetic unity of the building. After Hippolyte Flandrin, who had decorated such churches in the mid-nineteenth century, the leading artist to adopt these ideals was Puvis de Chavannes, and some of the broad patterns, subdued palette and suppressed detail that he chose for his decorations in secular buildings can be seen in the oil sketch he made for

58. Akseli Gallen-Kallela,
Lake Keitele, 1905.

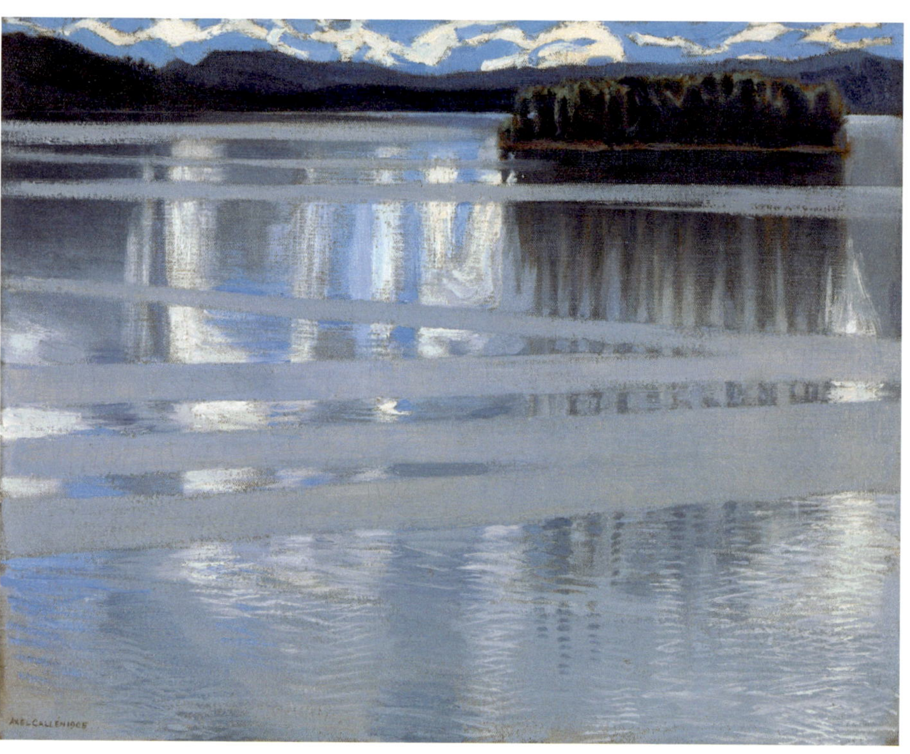

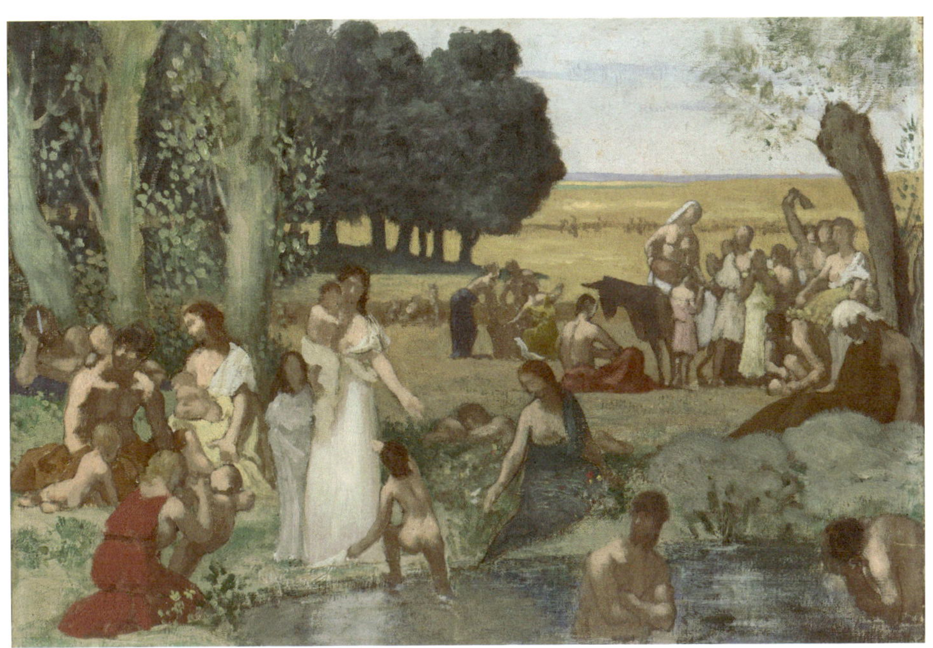

59. Pierre-Cécile Puvis de Chavannes, *Summer*, before 1873.

a huge canvas representing summer [59], which was exhibited in 1873. Paintings by Puvis had a huge influence on artists of a far less conservative temper, including Gauguin, Seurat and, later, Picasso.

Earlier in this book the height at which paintings were displayed was mentioned. There are of course many reasons why paintings are still hung far below the level the artist would have intended. The height of the room in which they are displayed is one factor. But there is also the indirect influence of a modern aesthetic entailing a strong, even puritanical, aversion on the part of the admirers of Cézanne and Van Gogh and Gauguin to the fiction of recession. 'Preserving the integrity of the picture surface' is a cliché that critics have used to validate much that is held to be canonical in modern painting, much that qualifies as truly modern. The veneration for Cézanne in particular not only stifles dispassionate evaluation of his paintings to a degree that is unprecedented in the history of Western art but has distorted our understanding of his predecessors, typified by the much-repeated misconception that his paintings have some profound affinity with those of Poussin. The structure of Poussin's paintings is solid, with every part complete and in a fixed relation to every other, as well as to the whole. The opposite is true of Cézanne's.

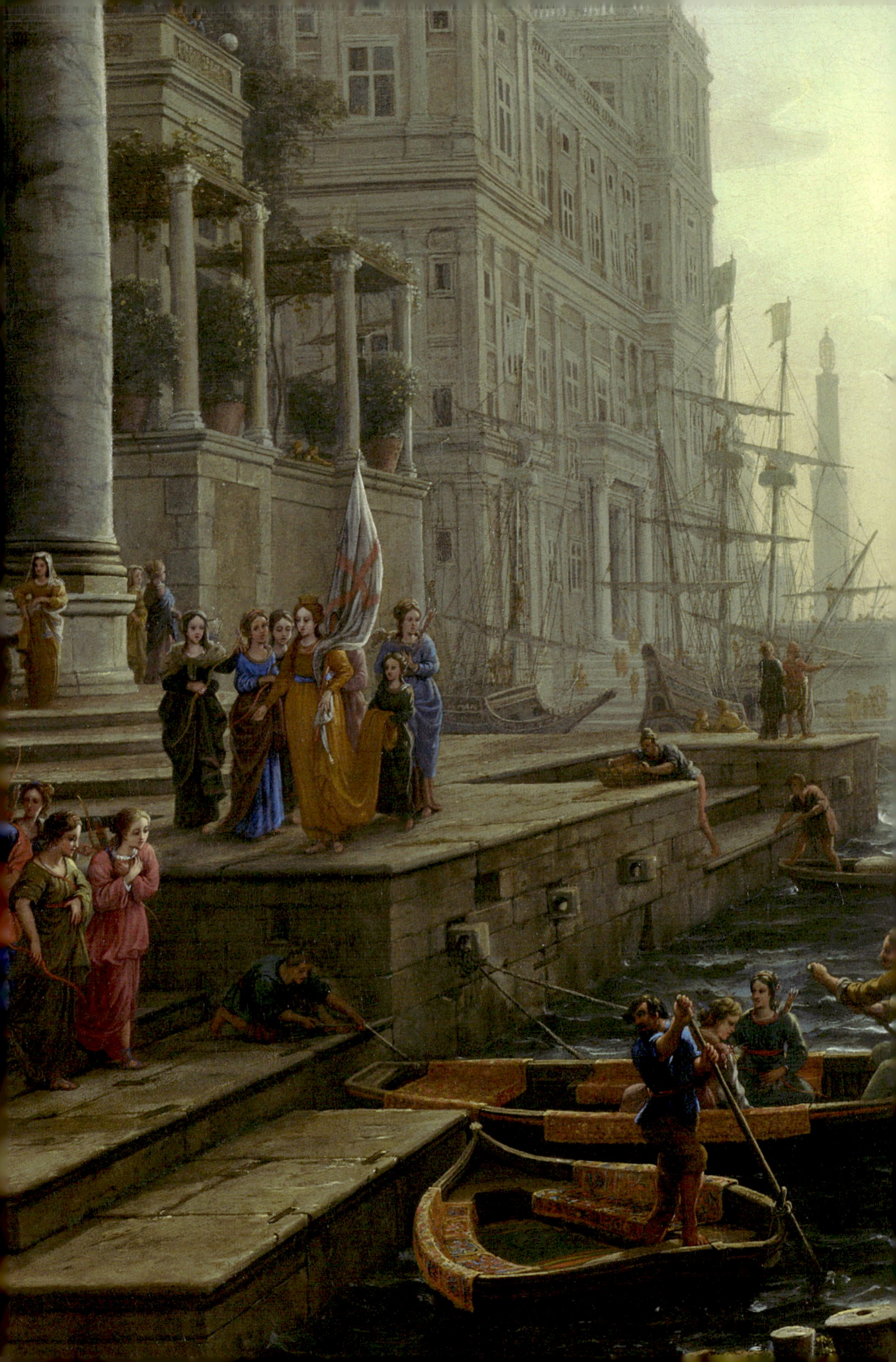

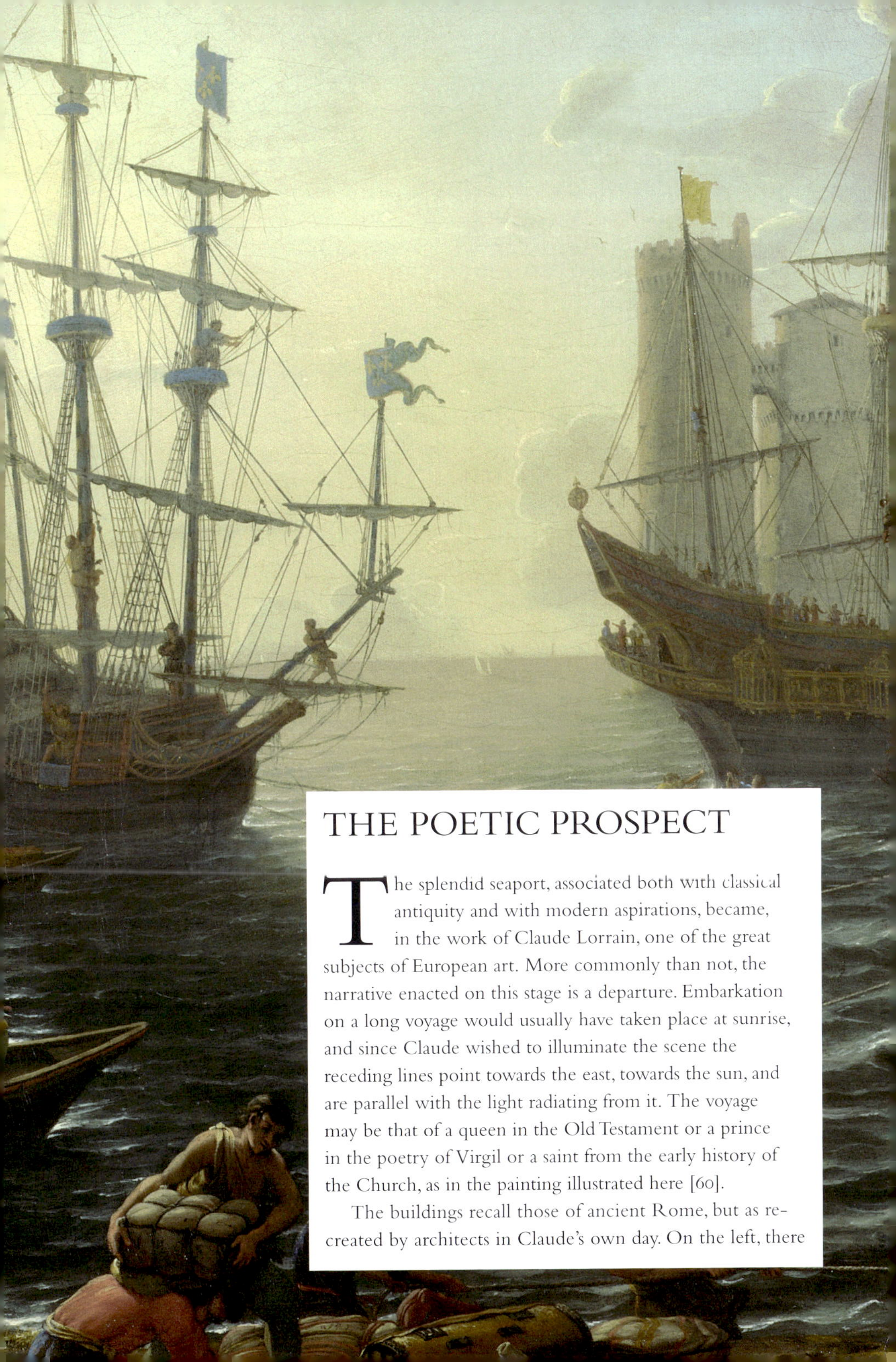

THE POETIC PROSPECT

The splendid seaport, associated both with classical antiquity and with modern aspirations, became, in the work of Claude Lorrain, one of the great subjects of European art. More commonly than not, the narrative enacted on this stage is a departure. Embarkation on a long voyage would usually have taken place at sunrise, and since Claude wished to illuminate the scene the receding lines point towards the east, towards the sun, and are parallel with the light radiating from it. The voyage may be that of a queen in the Old Testament or a prince in the poetry of Virgil or a saint from the early history of the Church, as in the painting illustrated here [60].

The buildings recall those of ancient Rome, but as re-created by architects in Claude's own day. On the left, there

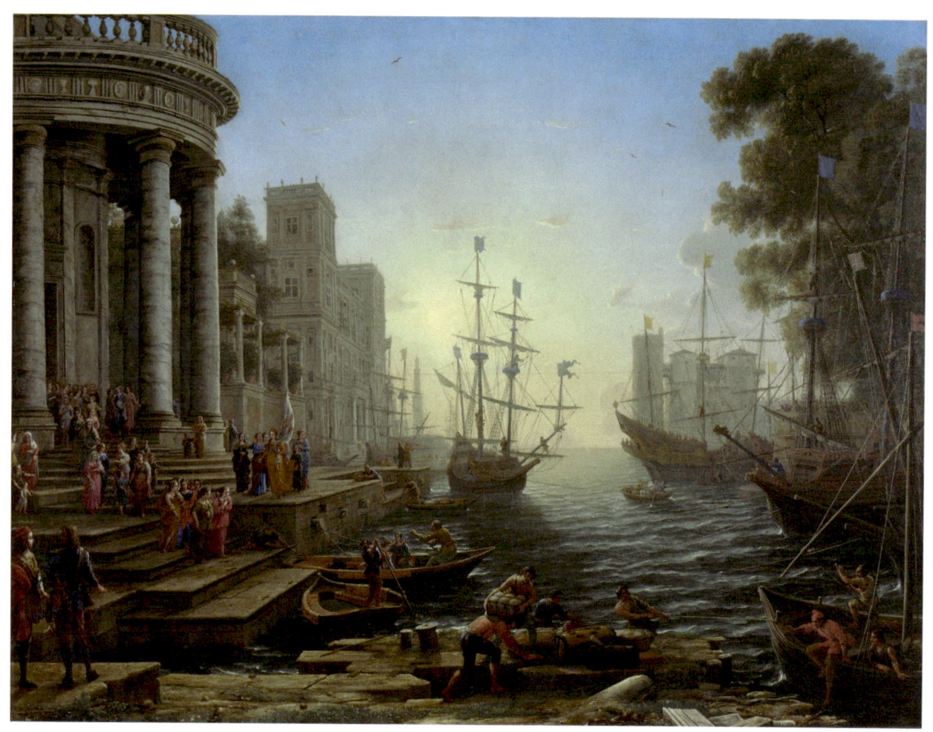

60 (and detail, previous pages).
Claude Lorrain, *Seaport
with the Embarkation of Saint
Ursula*, 1641.

is the stone quay; next, a great temple in the form of a rotunda
encircled by monolithic marble columns; then terraces and
hanging gardens with the colossal flowerpots (far larger than
any that can ever have been fired) much loved by this artist;
then a vast stone palace with corner towers; and, finally and
faintly, a tall round tower in two stages, crowned by a beacon.
There are buildings on the right as well, and trees with foliage
that seems as soft as the clouds behind, and a succession of
ships in which sailors can just be discerned climbing on the
rigging. And it could also be said that we are in this picture:
that is, we identify quite easily with the tall figures standing in
the extreme left foreground, witnessing the solemn procession
of Ursula and her escort of many near-identical virgins, all
bearing the emblems of their martyrdom (thus anticipating
their heavenly triumph). The future as well as the distance is
present in this painting.

Such paintings by Claude are not only poetic (often, in fact,
they were inspired by poetry); they also inspired poets. Father
Thames, in Alexander Pope's *Windsor Forest* (1712), invokes a
great Imperial port:

The painter who developed Claude's compositions and poetic conceptions in the most spectacular manner was J. M.W. Turner. He also recorded developments on the Thames which no one had foreseen. His *Rain, Steam and Speed – The Great Western Railway* [62], exhibited in 1844, depicts a steam train packed with passengers, hurtling over the Maidenhead viaduct (recently built to the design of the great engineer Isambard Kingdom Brunel). In the distance on the left we see an earlier feat of engineering, Sir Robert Taylor's road bridge of the 1770s. On the river, far below the viaduct, there is a pleasure boat, and to the right of the viaduct we can just discern a plough [61]. Boats and ploughs, ancient inventions, landmarks in the history of technology, are placed here to provide a historical context for the new invention of steam power. In addition, because their pace is slow they serve as a contrast for the speed that steam power has made possible. Everything in this painting is indistinct – the sturdy piers of the viaduct as well as the hare running in front of the train [63]. Turner wished to record the experience of trying to see things when we are moving at speed in bad weather, but to appreciate the originality of this work we should also reflect on how he has virtually eliminated the foreground. He was always interested in distance, in what can only be half-perceived, or discerned with difficulty. These are properties shared by dreams or by visions.

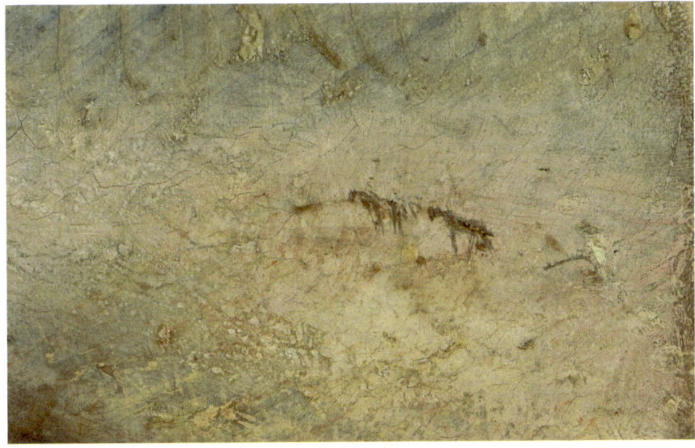

61 (detail) and 62 (overleaf). J.M.W. Turner, *Rain, Steam and Speed – The Great Western Railway*, exhibited 1844.

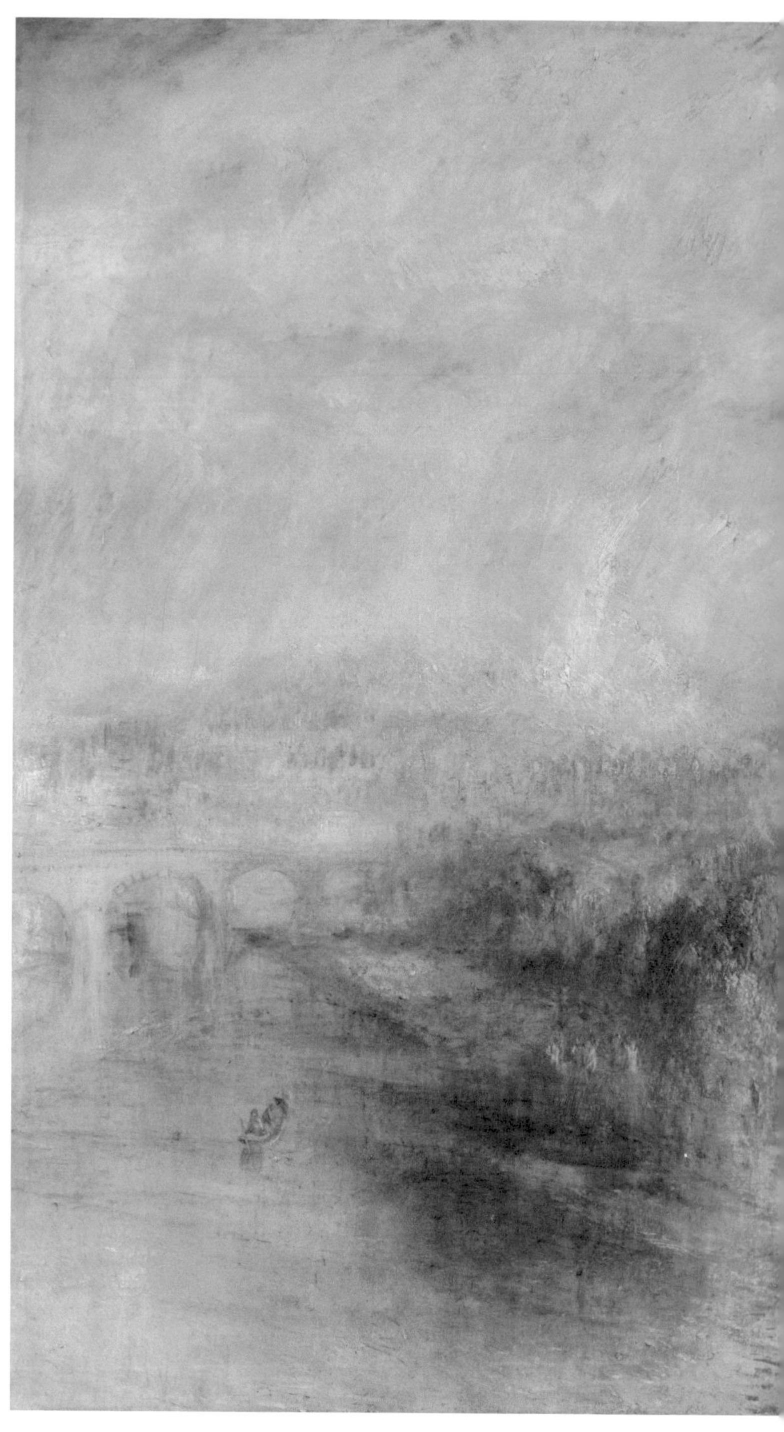

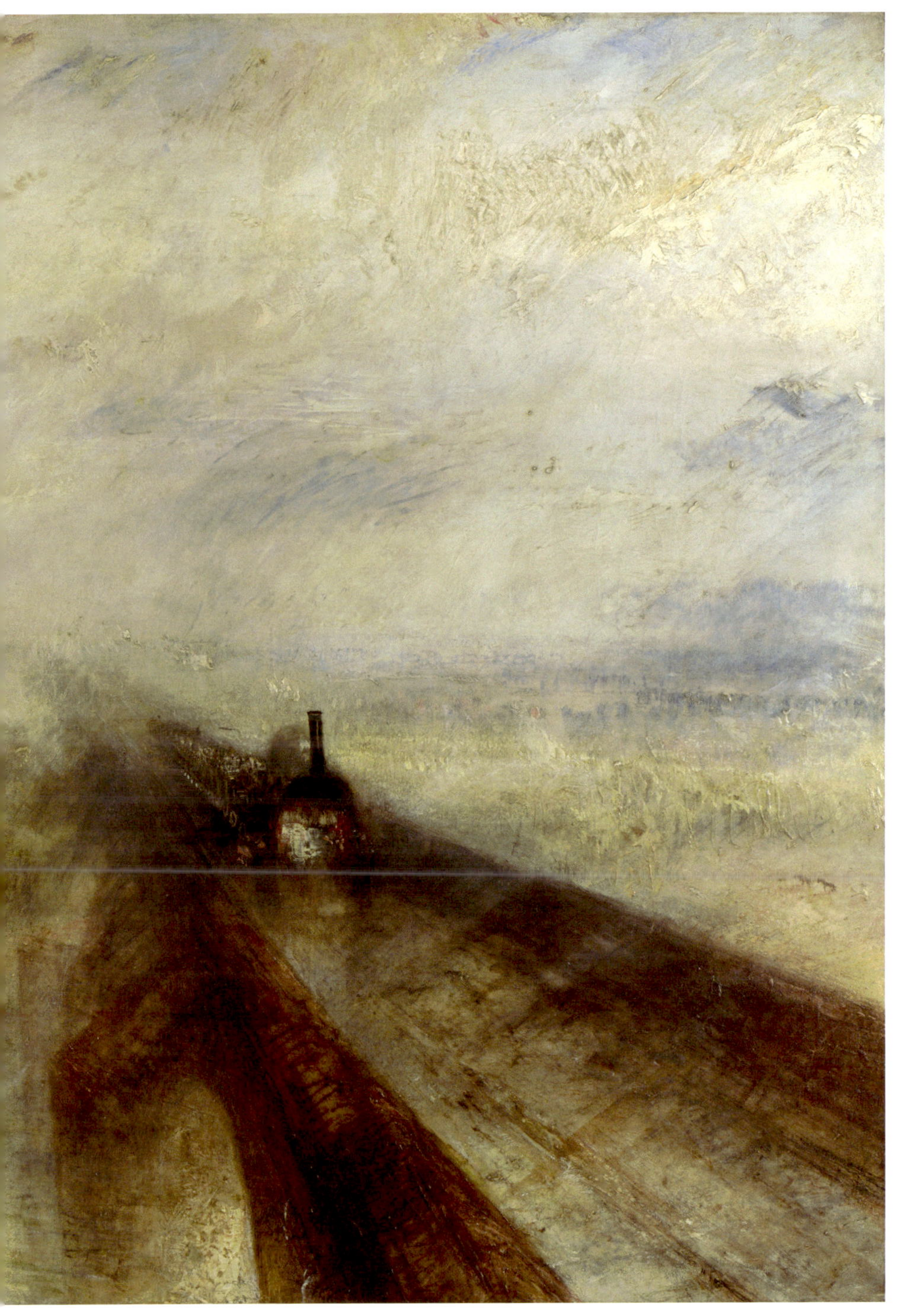

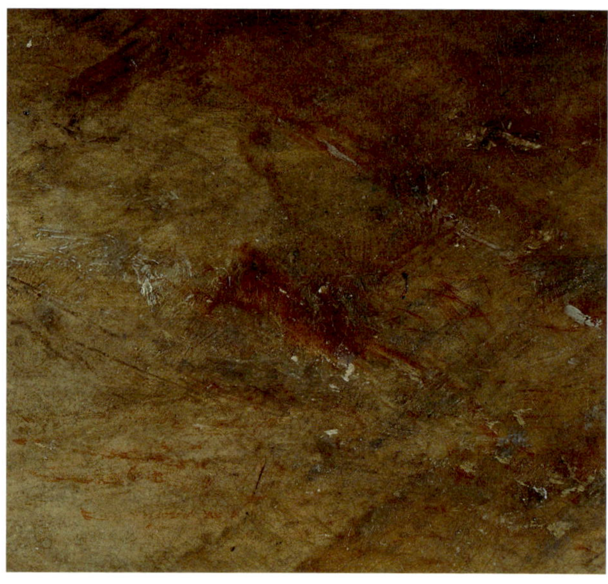

63. Detail from *Rain, Steam and Speed – The Great Western Railway.*

Rain, Steam and Speed was exhibited two years after the publication of Tennyson's *Locksley Hall*, in which the feverish narrator is both attracted and repelled by the 'heady dreams of progress … In the steamship, in the railway, in the thoughts that shake mankind', deciding, finally, that

> *Not in vain the distance beacons. Forward, forward let us range.*
> *Let the great world spin for ever down the ringing grooves of change.*

Description in poetry is almost always metaphorical, and metaphor is less common in painting than in poetry. Paths can often be found in paintings but we do not often think of them as representing the path of life, as they do in the opening lines of Dante's *Divine Comedy* or in Bunyan's *Pilgrim's Progress.* The idea is perhaps suggested, though, by Poussin's landscapes, as mentioned in a previous chapter (pages 62–3). There are other exceptions, such as Raphael's *Vision of a Knight* or Caspar David Friedrich's *Winter Landscape* [64].

The path in Friedrich's painting has been covered by snow but it must be indicated by the line of whiter snow that lies between the discarded crutches of a traveller who is now seated against a rock. In the fir trees before him there is a crucifix to which he prays for strength to continue his journey along the faint diagonal leading to the arched bridge, beyond which the slender iron pinnacles of a Gothic cathedral rise through the mist. The building may be no more than a vision of a heavenly prospect, but the conifer is somehow equated with it. The symbolism may seem strained – even to the point of absurdity – and the message rather trite, yet the way the mist, perhaps a snowfall, is rendered (minute touches of paint dabbed with a cloth), and the gradual lightening of the sky above, where a faint flush of dawn is traversed by a few streaks of cloud, redeems the picture.

Some objects in nature always excite an identification with humanity – objects to which a simile is silently but ineradicably attached. The best example is that of an ancient and very tall tree. Alexandre Calame's *At Handeck* [65, 66] depicts a conifer in the Bernese Alps. Its great height is enhanced by its relation to the surrounding mountains. Some of the dead branches are aligned with the fissures in the huge mass of granite behind it on the left, and the green foliage at the very top is contrasted with snow-covered peaks amid white clouds and small patches of blue sky. As we follow the dark trunk upwards we are also seeing further and further into the distance. A reverse progress is made by the white of broken water, melting from the high glaciers, and falling for miles down into the Haslital valley, where

64. Caspar David Friedrich,
Winter Landscape, probably 1811.

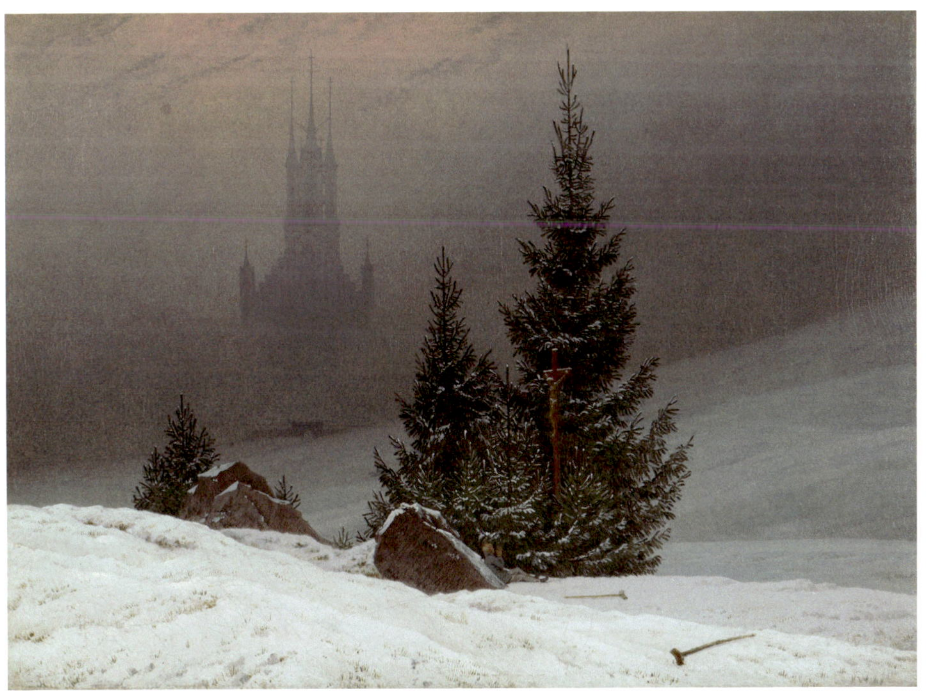

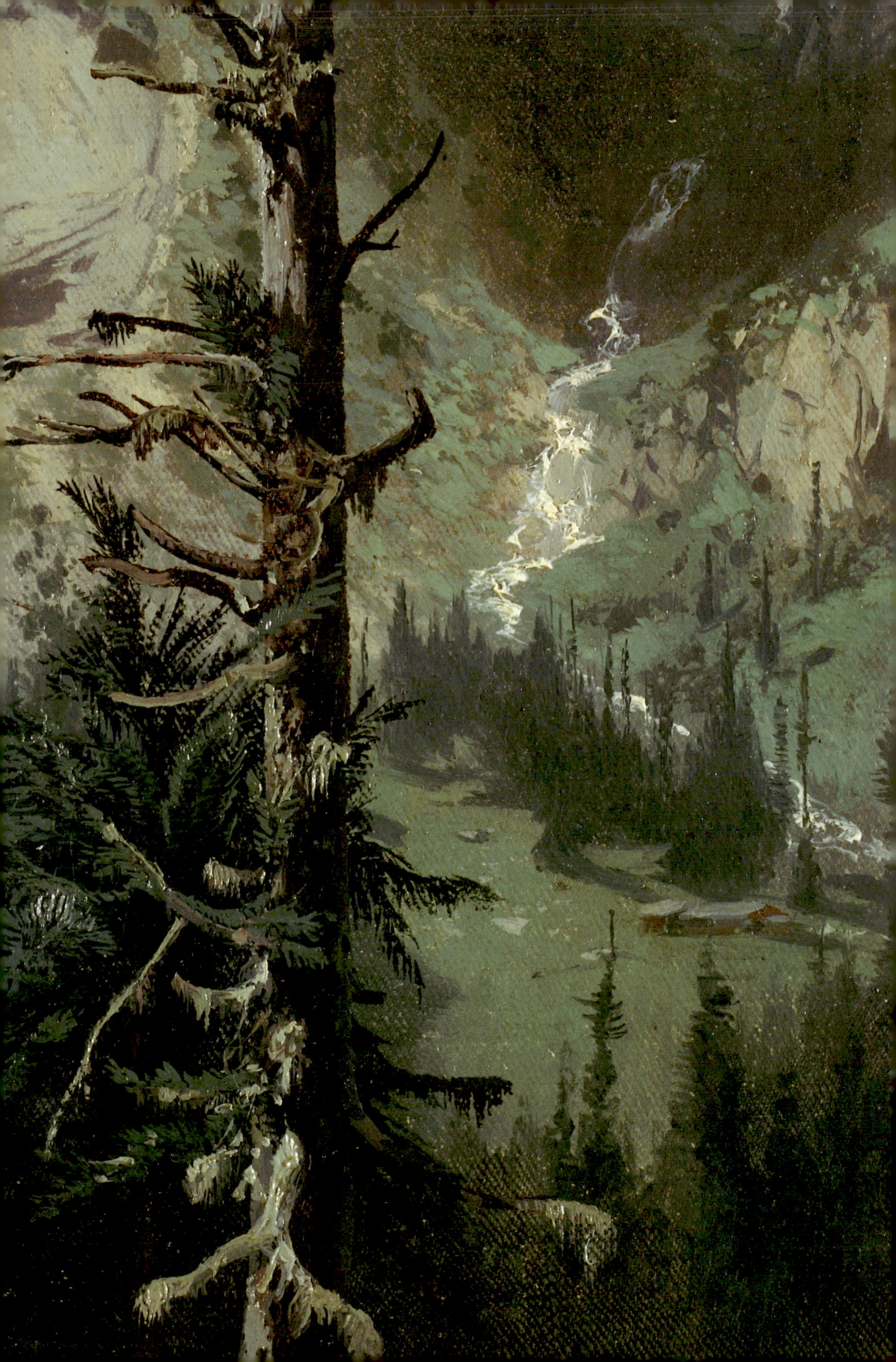

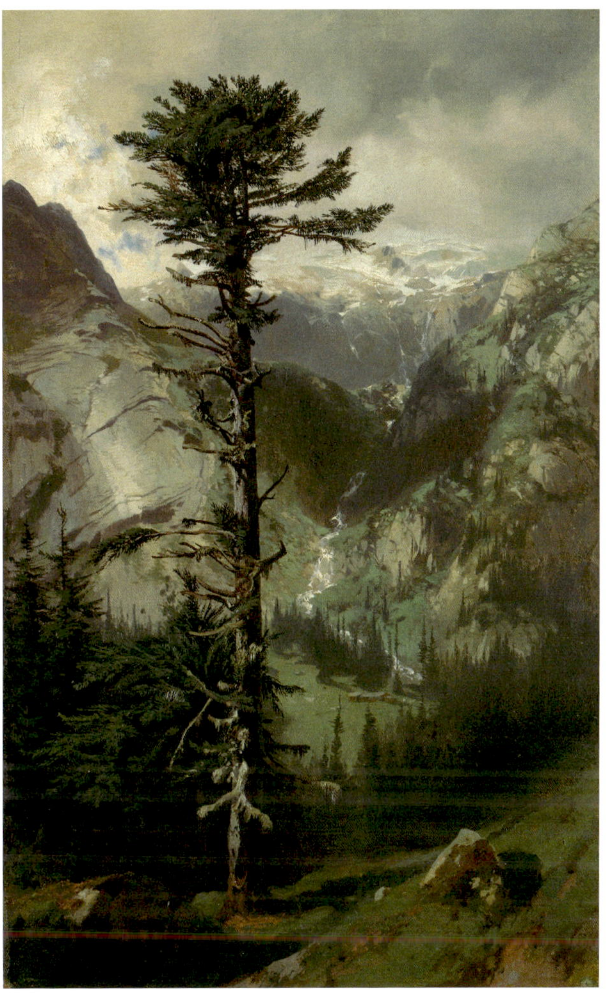

it forms a river, rendered in rapid lines of impasto, that rushes
past groves of pine and clustered chalets [65]. Calame's tree
means more to us than Friedrich's, precisely because it is not
explicitly symbolic, let alone part of a sermon, but both belong
to the period in which the conifer, in the form of the Christmas
tree, was adopted for a Christian festival.

Calame was an immensely successful painter in his lifetime
but he has long been neglected, probably because his subject
matter was later associated with the escapism of the popular
holiday brochure. The city itself had of course become more
alarming. *Men of the Docks* by George Bellows [67, 68] depicts
the port of Brooklyn, looking towards the shoreline of lower

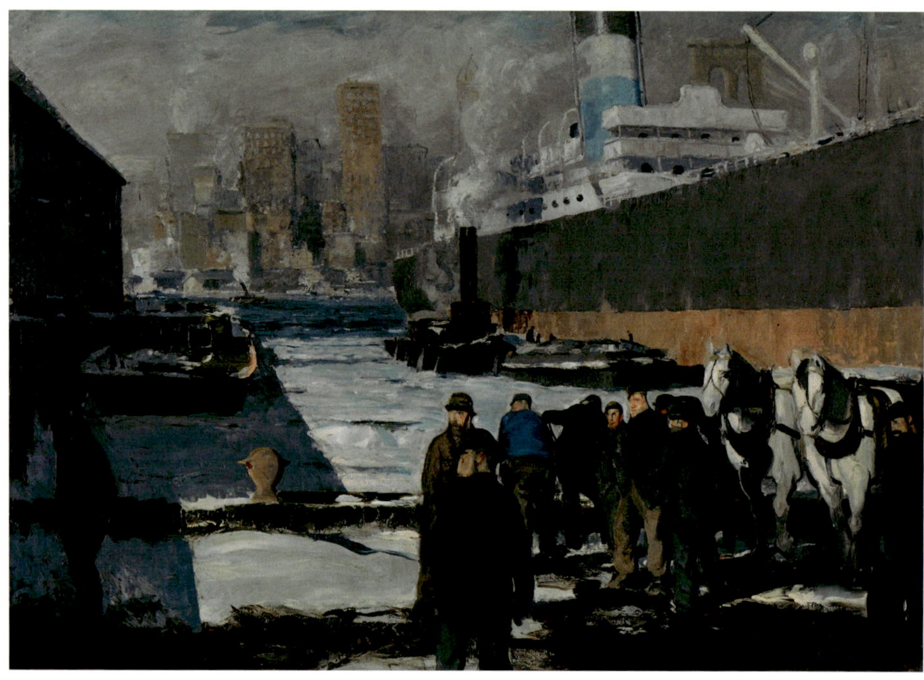

Manhattan in New York. The receding diagonals are deliberately violent and uncomfortable, those of the liner on the right matched by the darker grey, featureless building on the left and its still darker shadow. Since we are looking north and the shadows fall towards the right it must be late afternoon (during a New York winter it is not rare for snow and ice to melt very little during the course of the day). The painting is emphatically contemporary and realist, defying and denying all that is generally associated with poetry – the very reverse of the port scenes painted by Claude.

By deliberately limiting his palette the artist equates painted steel, rusty bollards and weather-beaten flesh. There is no delicacy of touch, no delightful transparency, only thick paint, some of it worked with a broad, stiff brush, but much of it applied with a palette knife, as in the steel flank of the ship where we find the characteristic ridge of paint at the edge of the surface flattened by the blade. But those diagonals conduct us into space, into the city of New York, then the fastest-growing metropolis in the world, with its towers half-obscured by mist and steam. It is not only the distance, it is the future, as menacing as the brutalised faces of the dockers, but with a real, albeit infernal, majesty.

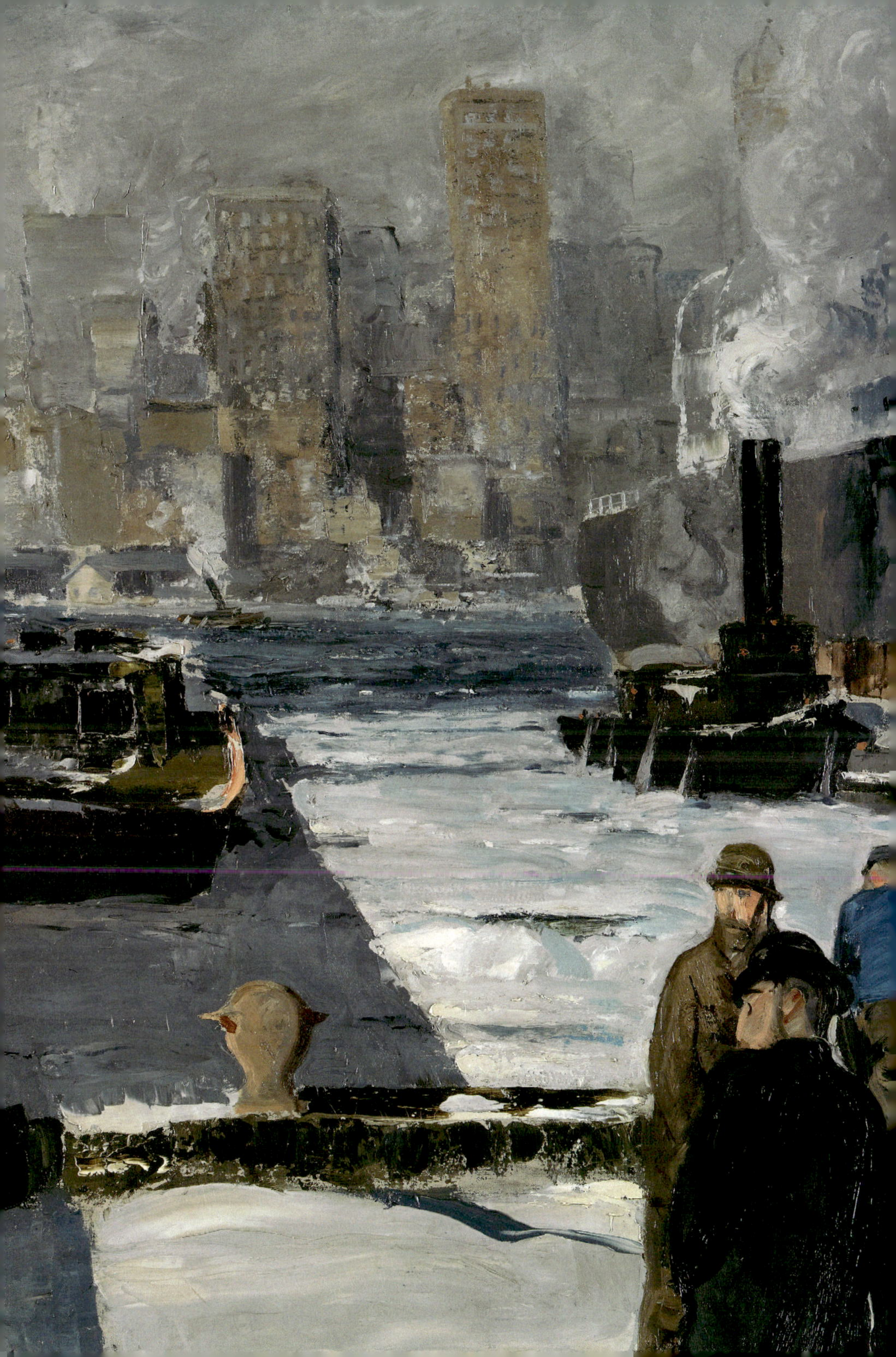

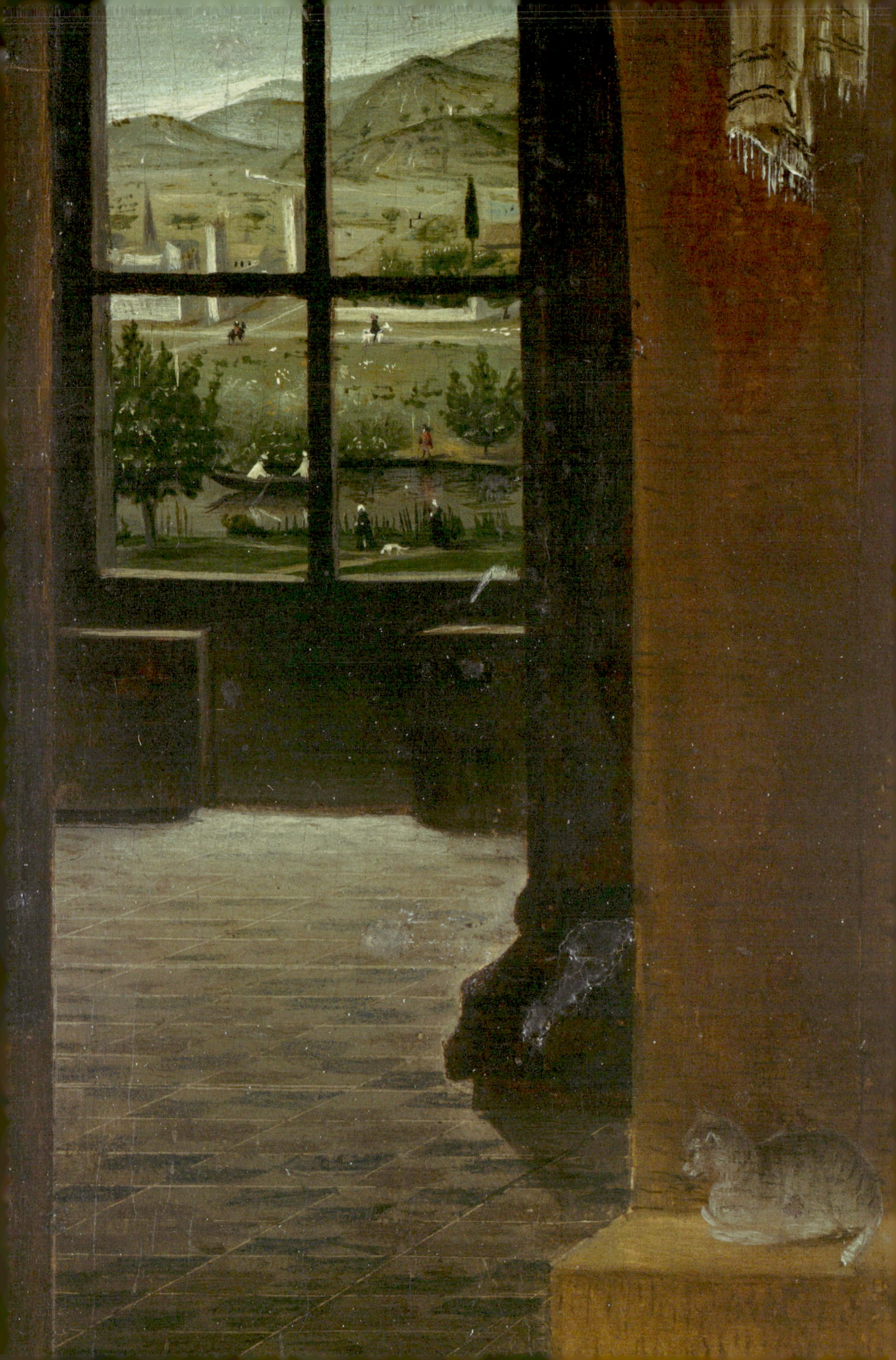

FURTHER READING

These notes are intended to help the reader discover more about the paintings illustrated, the poetry quoted and the ideas discussed in this book. Priority is given to texts in English which have been published relatively recently, many of them by the National Gallery. To find out more about particular artists see the Macmillan/Grove *Dictionary of Art* where notes on further reading are also provided.

In addition to the painting by **Petersen** [1] a collection of oil sketches formed by John and Charlotte Gere are on loan to the National Gallery. For an introduction to the purpose and popularity of such sketches see Christopher Riopelle, Xavier Bray and Charlotte Gere, *A Brush with Nature*, London 2003.

There is little here of a technical nature on **linear perspective** and its mathematical basis. The reader who wishes to explore the ways in which pictorial space was introduced into Italian art during the thirteenth, fourteenth and fifteenth centuries should read *The Birth and Rebirth of Pictorial Space* by John White, 3rd edition, London 1987. *Perspective in Perspective* by Lawrence Wright (London 1983) covers a broader field including, for example, architect's presentation drawings, the bird's-eye view, stage sets, photography and film. Its opening chapter provides a lively, often colloquial, occasionally whimsical introduction, emphasising how artificial the conventions of perspective really are.

69. Detail from Antonello da Messina, *Saint Jerome in his Study* (see fig. 20). The patterns of the floor tiles are characteristic of Naples, where Antonello is known to have worked, rather than Venice, where this is generally supposed to have been painted. It is the reflected light as well as the distance that renders the patterns illegible.

The lines from Shakespeare's historical romance **Cymbeline** (page 9), probably written in 1609 or 1610, come from act 1, scene 3, where Imogen interrogates Pisanio concerning the departure of Leonatus. It is a striking fact that this passage coincides in date with the first recorded use of the telescope.

For *Saint George and the Dragon* by **Uccello** [4] see Dillian Gordon, *National Gallery Catalogues: The Fifteenth-Century Italian Paintings*, vol. I, London 2003, pp. 398–405. Other scholars have favoured a much earlier date than that given here.

For the great altarpiece by **Lorenzo Monaco** [6], the side panels of which were the first examples of early Italian art to enter the National Gallery, see Gordon 2003, pp. 162–87. For *The Birth of the Virgin* by **Giovanni di Paolo** [8] and related panels from the same predella, see ibid., pp. 85–103.

The painting by the **Workshop of Campin** [9] is catalogued by Lorne Campbell in *National Gallery Catalogues: The Fifteenth-Century Netherlandish Paintings*, London 1998, pp. 83–91, where he persuasively argues that it is derived from a lost painting by Campin. Given the vanishing point to the left of the picture, it may be significant that another workshop painting derived from the same source forms the right wing of a diptych.

Ronald Lightbown's monograph on **Crivelli** includes a detailed discussion of *The Annunciation* [11], proposing many symbolic meanings as well as tracing the artist's sources (New Haven and London 2004, pp. 333–4).

A remarkable analysis of the compositional and perspectival devices – the visual rhymes, divisions and pointers – employed by **Gossaert** in his *Adoration* [12] is provided by Lorne Campbell on pp. 374–6 of his *National Gallery*

Catalogues: The Sixteenth-Century Netherlandish Paintings, London 2014.

For the theatrical aspect of this topic (page 29) see the painting associated with the Bibiena, the great Bolognese family of artists specialising in **stage sets and scenery painting**, entitled *The Interior of a Theatre* (probably 1700–50, NG 936, not normally on display but illustrated on the National Gallery website). It is unusual in representing the audience in a theatre as well as the stage. For *quadratura* (page 30) and its relationship to theatre architecture see also Wright 1983, chapter 6, cited under linear perspective, above.

A good introduction to **Canaletto** and Venetian view-painting in general [17, 18] is provided by Charles Beddington in *Venice: Canaletto and his Rivals*, London 2011. For the use by artists of **lenses and optical devices**, see Wright 1983, chapter 8, and also *Devices of Wonder* by Barbara Maria Stafford and Frances Terpak (Los Angeles 2001), especially pp. 307–13 for the camera obscura. Examples of the types of portable camera obscura artists are likely to have used in the seventeenth and eighteenth centuries can be seen in London's Science Museum and in the Museum of Scientific Instruments, Harvard University.

For Dutch seventeenth-century **peepshows** [21] (perspective boxes – 'an adult's spectacle-game'), only six of which survive, see Stafford and Terpak 2001, p. 107 and p. 238.

The most interesting example of the influence of **Vermeer** on photography (page 38) is the work of Charles Latham, who was much employed in the early twentieth century by the magazine *Country Life*. His photographs of the interiors of Lindisfarne Castle are especially fine examples.

The type of wood-carving in relief using separate planks which is mentioned in connection with the **Master of Saint Bartholomew** [25] is discussed in my *Materials of Sculpture*, London 1993, pp. 127–9.

Mantegna [27] by Ronald Lightbown (Oxford 1986) includes a valuable chapter devoted to this artist's 'paintings in monochrome' (pp. 210–18).

The use of **flower paintings** as overdoors is found in Italy and Spain by the mid-seventeenth century in the work of Mario de' Fiori and Juan de Avellano and remained popular in all parts of Europe for more than a century. The overmantel painting, combined with a mirror, seems to have been especially popular in Holland [29]. For **van Huysum** [30], see Paul Taylor's *Dutch Flower Painting 1600–1720*, London and New Haven 1995. He notes how the brilliant colours in the painting illustrated here are not arranged to enhance any sense of depth. His explanation for the two dates is that the artist had to delay finishing the painting because he wanted to add some flowers that were not in season. But that must have been a common problem and if the painting was not deemed to be complete why would the artist sign it?

For more on **Meléndez** [32] see William B. Jordan and Peter Cherry, *Spanish Still Life from Velázquez to Goya*, London 1995, pp. 152–63. The apparent projection out of the picture plane of a fruit basket, a fruit, a knife handle or a cloth is a recurring feature of European still-life painting from Caravaggio onwards.

When the Barbarigo portrait by **Titian** [35] was available for sale in Amsterdam in 1639 it seems to have been much admired by artists and its compositional formula, including the compelling projection of the elbow, was adopted by Rembrandt, firstly in an etched self portrait and then in the great painted self portrait dated 1640 (NG 692). The influence of Titian's painting can be traced in the work of other Dutch painters, most obviously Hals, but also Lievens, Mieris and Coques (see NG 2864, NG 1874 and NG 2527).

For a full account of *Whistlejacket* by **Stubbs** [36] see the entry by Judy Egerton in *National Gallery Catalogues: The British Paintings*, London 1998, pp. 240–7.

The subject of **Noli me tangere** [41] is the encounter between the risen Christ and Mary Magdalene, when Christ warns her not to touch him. This and earlier landscape paintings by **Titian** are admirably surveyed by Antonio Mazzotta in *Titian: A Fresh Look at Nature*, London 2012.

The best succinct account of the achievements of **Hobbema** [45] and **Ruisdael** [43] (especially the latter) is in the final section of the second chapter of Kenneth Clark's *Landscape into Art*, London 1949. Erika Langmuir's discussion of Hobbema's *Avenue at Middelharnis* is in the *National Gallery Companion Guide*, revised edition, London 2016, pp. 220–2.

Critical assessments of the achievements of the **Impressionists** are as rare as uncritical introductions to the work of the individual artists are common. The fifth chapter of Kenneth Clark's *Landscape into Art* has not been surpassed in this respect.

Alexander Pope's **Windsor Forest** (page 82) belongs to a tradition of landscape poetry which traces the course of a river as a way to connect political, mythological and topographical themes. The evocation of a great and prosperous city port comes at its climax, where the 'two fair cities' are London and Westminster. Whitehall takes its name from the use of Portland stone, the white limestone that was increasingly used for public buildings in London and which suited classical architecture based on prototypes of white marble.

For the *Seaport with the Embarkation of Saint Ursula* by **Claude** [60] see Humphrey Wine, *National Gallery Catalogues: The Seventeenth-Century French Paintings*, London 2001, pp. 94–103. It is one of three paintings of seaports by Claude in the National Gallery.

For *Rain, Steam and Speed* by **Turner** [62] see Egerton 1998, pp. 316–25, cited above under Stubbs.

Turner was himself a poet and was much inspired by Shelley. Tennyson's 'ringing grooves of change' has a bewildering and phantasmagoric character which perhaps deliberately recalls Shelley's metaphors and was thought by the poet to suit the deranged or at least inflamed mind of the narrator of **Locksley Hall** (page 86).

It is generally supposed that *Men of the Docks* by **Bellows** [67] shows the Brooklyn docks in the early morning. But we are facing north and the shadows fall to the right so this cannot be correct. For a survey of related works by Bellows, see the essay 'Life by the River 1908–1912' by Carol Troyen in *George Bellows*, exh. cat., London 2012, pp. 105–30.

ACKNOWLEDGEMENTS

The author is grateful to Mary Crettier not only for improvements to every page but for discussions in front of every painting in this book; to Pieter Biesboer who helped him with the intended location of the van Huysum; to Ray Watkins for many felicities in the design; to Sarah Derry who not only edited the text with special care but helped him to shape it and persuaded him to extend it; and to Jan Green who had the idea that he could and should write it.

A CLOSER LOOK

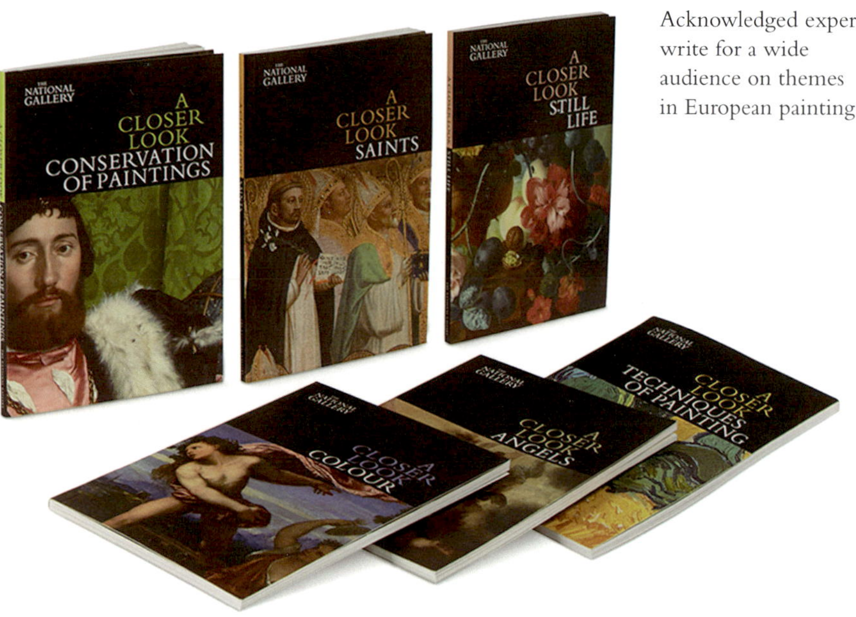

Acknowledged experts write for a wide audience on themes in European painting.

Allegory
Erika Langmuir
ISBN 9781857094855

Angels
Erika Langmuir
ISBN 9781857094848

Colour
David Bomford and Ashok Roy
ISBN 9781857094428

Conservation of Paintings
David Bomford, with Jill Dunkerton and Martin Wyld
ISBN 9781857094411

Deceptions & Discoveries
Marjorie E. Wieseman
ISBN 9781857094862

Faces
Alexander Sturgis
ISBN 9781857094640

Frames
Nicholas Penny
ISBN 9781857094404

Pictorial Space
Nicholas Penny
ISBN 9781857096163

Saints
Erika Langmuir
ISBN 9781857094657

Still Life
Erika Langmuir
ISBN 9781857095005

Techniques of Painting
Jo Kirby
ISBN 9781857095340

Visit the National Gallery Shop online to explore the series
www.nationalgallery.co.uk/products/art-books-series-a-closer-look

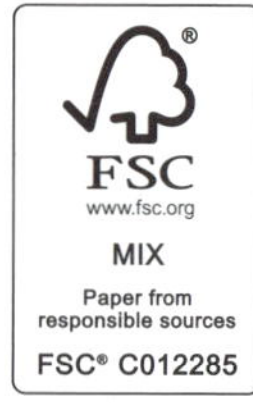